PRAISE FOR
CONFESSIONS OF A SERIAL ENTREPRENEUR

"Bill Canfield has developed a systematic and professional approach that will provide sure guidance for the prospective entrepreneur."

—John Prentis, former publisher, *St. Louis Globe-Democrat* and *World* magazine

"Bill gives us an authentic recounting of individual growth and extraordinary entrepreneurial success sustained by firm values, clarity of purpose, and personal discipline. Readers will learn about themselves and identify the self-sabotaging behaviors that prevent them from achieving their goals."

—Walter Metcalfe, attorney, board member of Financial Data Systems, *St Louis Post-Dispatch* Citizen of the Year

"Thought-provoking, heartfelt, and practical, *Confessions of a Serial Entrepreneur* is a must-read for any entrepreneur or business owner."

—Jack Hughes, marketing/advertising agency CEO of Hughes Advertising

"*Confessions of a Serial Entrepreneur* is an inspirational example of how spiritual commitment and values-based business principles can lead to tremendous business growth and financial success."

—Keith Graves, CFO, TALX Corporation

"*Confessions of a Serial Entrepreneur* is indispensable for anyone seeking to succeed at both business and life. Full of practical wisdom, thought-provoking principles, and invaluable first-hand experience, Bill Canfield provides a true north for aspiring entrepreneurs."

—Josh Crane, Head of School,
Stoney Brook School

CONFESSIONS OF A SERIAL ENTREPRENEUR

CONFESSIONS OF A SERIAL ENTREPRENEUR

*A Biography of Solving Business Problems
Using Technology, with a Management Style
Grounded in Faith*

BY BILL CANFIELD

© 2018 by Bill Canfield

All rights reserved. No part of this book may be reproduced or transmitted in any form or by any means, electronic or mechanical, including photocopying, recording, or by any information storage and retrieval system, except in the case of brief quotations embodied in critical articles and reviews, without prior written permission of the publisher.

Although the author and publisher have made every effort to ensure the accuracy and completeness of information contained in this book, we assume no responsibility for errors, inaccuracies, omissions, or any inconsistency herein.

Printed in the United States of America

Library of Congress Control Number: 2018934045

ISBN Paperback: 978-1-949639-87-2

Interior Design: Ghislain Viau

*To my fun and loving family,
and the wonderful people at TALX*

CONTENTS

Acknowledgements..............................xi
Major Events in My Life........................xiii
Introduction: A Surprise Letter...................1
Chapter 1 | Foundations........................5
Chapter 2 | Into the Unknown..................15
Chapter 3 | Competing........................27
Chapter 4 | A Decision that Changed Everything...41
Chapter 5 | The Main Thing....................47
Chapter 6 | Putting the Team Together..........55
Chapter 7 | Music in My Soul..................63
Chapter 8 | X's and O's.......................71
Chapter 9 | Providence........................79
Chapter 10 | Into the Public Arena..............91
Chapter 11 | A Stroke of Genius!...............103
Chapter 12 | A "SaaS-y" Connection.............109

Chapter 13 | Hitting a Home Run! 111

Chapter 14 | The TALX Way. 121

Chapter 15 | Hanging Up My Spikes 127

Chapter 16 | The Second Half 129

Chapter 17 | Doggin' It!. 137

Chapter 18 | Gratitude Attitude 143

ACKNOWLEDGEMENTS

I'd like to express my gratitude to my wife Sally, for her inspiration, guidance, and editing.

To my sons, Jim and Tom, for family editing.

To Melody Meiners, who organized much of the content.

To Keith Graves, for editing and timeline accuracy.

To Jack Hughes, for early encouragement to write this book.

To BusinessGhost, for editing, guidance, and management of the production aspects.

And finally, to Linda Currier, who kept me on-time and organized for more than forty years.

MAJOR EVENTS IN MY LIFE

1939   Born on January 2 in St. Louis, Missouri

1957   Graduated from Webster Groves High School

1961   Graduated from Purdue University with a bachelor's degree in Electrical Engineering (BSEE)

1961   Married Sally Martin, my high school sweetheart

1962   Graduated from Washington University with a master's degree in Business (MBA)

1962   Began my first "real" job with IBM in St. Louis, Missouri

1962–3 Served six months in the military

1964   Jim was born on March 25

1966   Tom was born on April 12

1968	Started my first company, Financial Data Systems (FDS)
1970	Sold FDS to Continental Telephone
1970	Bought a stone house at 620 N. Taylor in Kirkwood, Missouri, our home for 42 years
1972	Bought FDS back from Continental Telephone
1980	Sold FDS to Citicorp
1980	Started the first chapter of K-Life
1980	Became a Christian, accepting Jesus Christ as my personal Savior, joining Sally
1981	Founded Intech Group
1983	Founded Noetic Technologies
1987	Sold Noetic Technologies to MacNeal-Schwendler
1988	Bought a portion of Interface Technology from MiTek Industries and became its president
1990	Son Tom married Beth Dunaway in June
1991	Changed the name of Interface Technologies to TALX
1992	Son Jim married Nancy Scaggs in March; Sally and I became instant grandparents of Jenna, 13, and Derek, 10

MAJOR EVENTS IN MY LIFE

1992 Beth died of pancreatic cancer in August

1993 Granddaughter Becky was born to Jim and Nancy in January

1993 Son Tom married Weezie Skimming in December

1995 Grandson Sam was born to Tom and Weezie in May

1995 TALX built and began selling employment and income verification service called The Work Number

1996 Grandson Eddie was born to Jim and Nancy in March

1996 Granddaughter Annie was born to Tom and Weezie in May

1996 October 23, TALX went public on the NASDAQ, selling at $9 per share

1997 Investment community was disappointed in our performance, dropping our share price to below $3 per share

1998 Grandson Willie was born to Tom and Weezie in January

2001 Grandson Jack was born to Tom and Weezie in April

2001 September 11; I, along with six other TALX employees, was in New York City when the towers were hit

2001	Class-action lawsuit filed against TALX for misrepresentation
2002	SEC filed charges against TALX and levied fines against our CFO and me
2002	Acquired two unemployment processing companies on the same day, doubling TALX's annual revenues
2005	Joined the Board of The Magic House, St Louis Children's Museum
2005	SEC charges settled; I paid my SEC fine
2007	Equifax bought TALX for approximately $150 per share, on an adjusted basis
2008	Became Chairman of the Board of The Magic House
2009	Had two major surgeries on my back
2010	Retired from Equifax
2012	Founded the not-for-profit St. Louis Bridge Center
2013	Began developing residential homes in Naples, Florida

Introduction
A SURPRISE LETTER

In July of 2010, a few months after I had retired from TALX, I was going through my mail and came upon a letter from an employee, Steve Williams. Steve was a few days shy of his twelfth anniversary with TALX, and, like many people who worked there, Steve and I had sat down periodically to talk about his career and growth within the company.

I always enjoyed reading letters from employees who took time to just say thanks or let me know how their time at TALX had affected their lives. However, this letter in particular stood out to me. Steve wrote:

"As president of TALX, you set the tone by establishing the vision and the culture. Here are some of the things I've valued most under your leadership:

- Commitment to character and integrity
- Accountability for results
- Concern for individuals
- An intentional effort to serve and better our community
- Learned how to give back through company charitable foundation
- Freedom to fail/opportunity to succeed
- A positive, Christ-honoring environment
- Celebration of success

Also, as a die-hard Cardinals fan, it's been tremendous fun to work for someone who knows and loves baseball."

Steve closed his letter by thanking me for staying with the company after the sale to Equifax to ensure a smooth transition. I folded the letter up and laid it on my desk, and it struck me that this was perhaps the first time I'd seen a list that captured the culture, business principles, and people of TALX so precisely.

This made me curious. Was TALX unique? What did other employees think? I set about pulling together a list of eleven people who had been with the company for at least fifteen years. I scheduled interviews with each one of them, and when they walked into my office, I started the conversation by saying, "You have worked at TALX for [number, e.g., fifteen] years. What is it about the company culture and work environment that have enabled you to stay this long?"

A SURPRISE LETTER

I listened to everyone as they talked about their experiences with TALX and their individual reasons for staying with the company. During our discussions, I noticed that, while there was some variation in the number and content of answers, there were ten values common to everyone's responses.

TALX employees:

1. have the freedom to fail;
2. want to work with good people;
3. receive encouragement to be creative, innovative, and to take ownership;
4. like that TALX is growing, never static;
5. are given autonomy to work in their own way;
6. have visible leadership that lacks hierarchy, and are encouraged to express their opinions;
7. are trusted and respected to do the right thing, not micromanaged;
8. have a standard of excellence that gives people a sense of obligation and desire to do the right thing;
9. are empowered to take as much responsibility as they want; and
10. are focused on solving business problems by doing the right things for the right reasons, not just to please or look good for someone.

As I looked at this list, it became apparent to me that what they had described was a culture rooted in bringing together good people who endeavored to do business God's way. My experiences at TALX, and even earlier, had helped me to see that by doing business using God's principles, my passion was increased while employees also felt valued, and, in turn, God was honored.

My faith journey began in the early 1980s, leading me not only to a personal relationship with Christ, but also to an understanding of how the truths in the Bible affected me personally, including the business.

Not long after I had pulled together the list of values, many of which had been influenced by my faith, I retired from Equifax, now the owner of TALX. As I walked out the doors and into the next phase of my life, I left in place an organization teeming with bright individuals and an environment where innovation thrived. Opening that letter from Steve had crystallized those values in my mind, reminding me also of the faith journey that proved to be the genesis of much of my management philosophy. I have kept those interviews and the letter from Steve in a file as a reminder to me, but also as a catalyst to share with other entrepreneurs interested in learning about them, and, perhaps, in seeking the person of Jesus, who made all the difference.

Chapter 1
FOUNDATIONS

The Canfield family didn't simply go on vacation; we conquered vacation. From the moment we eased onto the nearly deserted, early morning highway, until the moment the white stone front of our house came back into view, we approached family trips with the energy, focus, and determination due any worthwhile venture.

We were ready to leave town before the joggers started pounding the pavement and the distant white noise of the early morning commute began, with all our luggage and the fold-out mattress from a sofa or a couple of plump beanbag chairs loaded in the back of our van. Well, at least the boys, Jim and Tom, and I were, but we waited on Sally, my wife. True, we owed her a debt of gratitude for the weeks she spent planning and packing for everyone, but we always found ourselves holding the keys while she checked and double-checked that we had absolutely everything we could potentially need. Invariably, I had to remind her that in the unlikely event we forgot something, we could buy it when we got there. "Let's just go."

"Once upon a time" wasn't just how many stories began. It was the opening line for many of our family vacations. And one thing was certain: Sally always made sure we were well prepared for whatever adventure awaited us on the other side of the drive.

Our major road trips were either to the sandy beaches of Sanibel Island, Florida, or to a condominium on the powdery slopes of Snowmass, Colorado. Both trips were more than fifteen hours away by car, and we rarely traveled any other way. Jim and Tom joked that I took a measure of pride in driving twenty-two hours and only stopping twice along the way. There was a seed of truth in that, as in most every joke. While we were never on the road for twenty-two hours, I will admit, Sally and the boys learned to be mindful of their water intake when we were traveling because, as they often heard, "We do not stop." Sally would pack a cooler she placed between the front seats, with drinks and the ingredients for sandwiches. She served lunch, so we didn't need to waste time stopping to eat.

Unplanned bathroom and snack breaks weren't the only diversions I discouraged. Along the way, we passed many monuments, museums, and historical landmarks, which I playfully referred to as "hysterical markers."

Sally would say, "Did you see that, Bill? We're going to pass the Grand Canyon in just a few miles. Why don't we stop and see it?" But . . . on we drove!

More than likely Sally had already seen whatever landmark we were approaching. On Sally's family vacations, something as small as a plaque on a barren landscape would have her dad pulling to the side of the road, no matter how minor the historical significance. But when I was behind the wheel, I had to remind everyone that there was the driving, and then there was the vacation, and the two did not mix. If we wanted to see the Grand Canyon, we would plan a trip to see the Grand Canyon, and they should just sit back and relax until our next stop, in about an hour and a half.

We were on a mission.

Jim and Tom would say we were racing the wind, and it was lost on no one that another driver passing us was the exception, not the rule. In addition to our economical use of stops, we also used our trusty CB radio to get us there quickly and efficiently. I would depress the button on our radio, use my handle, "Willy Wonka," and question the truck drivers about traffic conditions ahead. We would listen to their chatter to identify radar traps down the road. Without the diversions of mobile devices to distract the boys, driving easily became boring, but listening to the CB entertained them. When the radio wasn't enough, we played the alphabet game, or searched for state license plates, or kept our eyes peeled, so we didn't miss licking our thumbs and smacking our palms for good luck when we passed a white horse in a pasture.

Keeping them busy was a task, and handheld games weren't the only thing we didn't have. At that time seat belts weren't standard in cars, so when the boys got bored, they would be all over the back of the van, lounging on the mattress or beanbags or engaged in hand-to-hand combat. Sally spent equal parts of the drive watching the scenery and stretched around the side of her seat, almost endlessly repeating, "Stop it, boys."

I handed down the mantle of serious vacation driving to my boys, the very same one I received from my dad, Weldon Canfield. When I was growing up, every summer after school let out, my parents, my younger brother Tom, and I would set off on a family vacation. Summer after summer we traveled the country in a shiny new car, and by the time we were out of high school, we had seen most of the forty-eight contiguous states from the pristine leather seats of the newest Ford Thunderbird or Mustang, due to the clever thinking of my father.

Flying in the 1950s was expensive, so a long-distance vacation was a luxury for most families. My parents lived through the Great Depression, and the lean rationing of World War II that followed in its wake had taught them to make the most of the resources they had by being creative and frugal. That sensibility stuck with them long after the economy recovered. Dad came up with a brilliant plan that allowed us to travel all over the country while only paying half the typical airfare costs, and without putting a single mile on our family car. He would go to the local Ford dealership and pick up a new car the dealer needed to be delivered out of state. We would drive it across the country, where we would vacation before dropping it off and flying back home.

Dad followed an ironclad driving routine during our family car trips. Like the routine Sally and I followed with our boys, Dad got us up and out the door before the summer sun rose. Before leaving, he calculated the one-hundred-mile mark, and that was where we made our first stop of the day and ate breakfast. Fast-food restaurants did not line every interstate, so we spent the better part of an hour eating and stretching our legs before we got back in the car. We were on the road for the next 150–200 miles until we needed to fill up on gas, and once those doors clapped closed and the engine turned over, we would be off for another 150–200 miles.

We stayed that course until four in the afternoon, when we stopped at a motel to swim in the pool, eat dinner, and sleep. The next morning, we were up before the sun and back on the road. Once we pulled into the city where we were delivering the car, we vacationed for a week or ten days. The final day we would deliver the car to the dealer, dressed in our

Sunday best, Dad in a suit and Mom in a lovely dress, ready to make the flight home. The 1950s were called the golden age of air travel, and flying was considered a privilege. That meant you put on your business clothes before boarding. No sloppy dress!

Sally and I were both blessed to be able to travel often with our parents and privileged to be able to share that important tradition with our boys. We both grew up listening to stories about our family backgrounds and legacies, which instilled in us a deep sense of the importance of family. The days we spent with our parents, and later our boys, miles away from the routine of work and household responsibilities, helped shape our most cherished family memories.

***

Though vacations offered us a break from our day-to-day routines, they were never about lazily lying on a beach with our brains in the "off" position. Working hard always meant playing hard as far back as I could remember, and that was never more apparent than during the summer trips I took as a child to the Worthington Family Farm.

My mom, Jean Worthington Canfield, would pack my brother and me into our family car and drive every summer to her hometown of Washington Courthouse, Ohio. There we would spend a few weeks at the farm that had been in her family for generations.

FOUNDATIONS

Mom came from an Ohio family of politicians and bankers. We were a few generations removed from one of the state's more renowned political figures, Thomas Worthington. As one of the two first US senators from Ohio, he was part of the Constitutional Convention and played a pivotal role in bringing the state into the Union in 1803. He went on to serve as one of the first senators to the national Congress and then became the sixth governor of Ohio. For his role in the Constitutional Convention, he was awarded a land grant out of Washington, DC, which became the forty-thousand-acre Worthington farm estate. Through the generations, the property was divided, and eventually, Mom and my Aunt Edith inherited one thousand acres of the original rich, Ohio farmland. The home belonging to the original land grant remained intact as a national monument and museum, called Adena, which is still located in Chillicothe, Ohio.

While Aunt Edith moved to the farm after she was married, Mom got married and stayed closer to the city. Aunt Edith was the picture of a sturdy, farming matriarch, raising and training trotting horses. It was hard physical work. Mom, on the other hand, was always the more winsome and genteel of the two sisters, sharp-witted and a prolific reader. She preferred being inside to working outside. However, getting the house cleaned and dinner prepared was no small task on the farm, which had electric lights but no indoor plumbing.

We bathed in the frigid waters pumped from the well, and we disliked using an outhouse in the middle of the night. One summer we arrived to find that the hand pump in the kitchen had been replaced with a faucet and running water. Eventually, the luxury of an indoor bathroom came to the farm, but by that time I was off to college and my visits were fewer.

During my summers on the farm, I began to understand the value of hard work and the satisfaction of doing a good job. On those summer days when we weren't on the farm or traveling, I kept myself busy at home doing jobs like cutting grass for the neighbors. Eventually, my dad found a job for me in the shipping department at the company where he worked, Sporlan Valve, an engineering start-up that designed, manufactured, and sold air conditioner components. My job was to assemble bulb clamps, a somewhat tedious undertaking that required me to put two pieces of metal together with two small bolts and nuts and place them in a little brown envelope. I sat alone in our basement day after day, giving the job my complete focus and attention. My goal was to fill enough envelopes to earn $1 per hour, and I was thrilled when I streamlined the task enough to earn $1.25 per hour. I passed all of these to my son Jim, when he was old enough.

One summer after Sally and I began dating in high school, her parents paid me to wash their windows. I didn't stop until I had conquered those windows, and they were the cleanest in the neighborhood. For days afterward, her parents told their friends how impressed they were with my work.

Some jobs are worth much more than a paycheck, and, as Sally told it, my work ethic and manners were part of the reason her parents encouraged our dating. My Dad taught me always to give 100 percent effort, and I seldom approached anything halfway. I always believed in approaching vacations and work with equal intensity, because, generation after generation, being a Canfield has meant working hard as well as playing hard.

Chapter 2
INTO THE UNKNOWN

Businesses and the people who run them have always fascinated me. When I meet another business person, I love hearing them talk about their business model, products, revenue stream, hiring practices, and so on. I usually find that the person I'm asking enjoys talking about what they do, and how they do it, as much as I enjoy hearing about it.

My father nurtured my early interest in business at our dinner table. As happens at many start-ups, my dad wore many hats for Sporlan, but he was primarily the business manager, overseeing everything except engineering and sales. He worked hard to manage the operations of the firm, but he always made it home in time to join us for dinner. We sat around the table listening to him talk about the day's business and growth, and what he'd read in the business pages of the *St. Louis Post-Dispatch* about the city's thriving banking, brewing, and engineering firms. We talked about and speculated on the performance of his investments, and those conversations developed my interest in learning more about the stock market. My dad loved business! By the time I left for college, I understood the risks and rewards of business and had a financial vocabulary.

Early in my college years, I told my dad I wanted to learn more about the stock market, so he put a call in to a stockbroker friend of his who took me on as a summer worker. My job of running mail, doing errands, and the like gave me time to listen and learn how the market operated. Options trading fascinated me, and I opened my first stock brokerage account and began trading options. While I only earned minimum wage, one dollar an hour, I left that job with an understanding of how I could make money using my knowledge alone. A few years later, after we both graduated from college and Sally and I married, I used the profits from my options trading while in college to buy her an engagement ring. Even though I had an engineering degree, I felt sure I wanted to pursue a business career. Newly married, I returned to school to complete the MBA I had started in the summer after graduation from Purdue.

You could say entrepreneurialism runs in my blood. My grandfathers and great grandfathers carved enterprising paths for themselves in politics, banking, and manufacturing. Mom delighted in talking about the Worthington family and their role in history and industry, and we loved hearing about the visionary ideas they had and how they saw these ideas to fruition. Our great, great great-uncle, Thomas Worthington, had helped shape the state of Ohio as a senator and governor, and our trips to the family farm were always a reminder of his dedication and wisdom.

My grandfather, William Worthington, started Fayette County Bank in Washington Courthouse, Ohio, where he served as president for most of his life. He had a well-deserved and far-reaching reputation for being an insightful, smart, and trustworthy business person. Though he and my grandmother, Mepah, died before Tom and I were born, Mom and Aunt Edith often told us about the influence they had on their lives in Washington Courthouse.

Decades after they were gone, their influence lived on in the town. When we went to the farm for our summer stays, the local papers would run a little blurb about my mom's visit. The family lessons about the values of education, leadership, dedication, and vision underpinned the stories of our family, and they made a lasting impression on me.

Dad's family history was a bit more colorful. A few rascals branched off his family tree—gamblers, card players, and the like. Dad's family hailed from Detroit, Michigan, the birthplace of the assembly line and the center of the booming auto industry in the early twentieth century. Detroit's prime location on the water made it a hub for trade and commerce, and it was fertile ground for enterprising businesses and salesmen catering to the auto industry. When the assembly line drove down the costs of vehicle manufacturing, the proliferation of cars across the country got underway. The demand for raw materials, like rubber, grew. My granddad, Neil Canfield, was a travelling rubber salesman for Gates Rubber when this supply and demand began to intersect. In a sense, he was an entrepreneur.

My first job out of college was with IBM as a systems engineer, and I was teamed up with a talented salesperson named Bob Fischer. Bob would sell, and I would work with the customer to implement what he had sold. Bob sold a 1440 computer system to First National Bank in St. Louis. The bank was going to use the system to service savings and loan associations. I led a team of several programmers from the bank assigned to build a software package that automated manual paper transactions done by tellers. This was to be an online system, one of the first systems of its kind in the country. While working for IBM, I had an office at the bank. I spent over a year working with the bank and local savings and loan associations to determine what the system needed to do. I spent the next eighteen months in developmental mode, guiding and creating the programs used to run the application. The software package we built accomplished several goals: It expedited the transaction process, it decreased the margin of error, and it recorded every transaction on a master file for later accounting and statement processing. To the savings and loan associations, time saved and errors eliminated were dollars and cents. The financial industry desperately needed this application, and First National Bank capitalized on that demand by selling, with my help, the completed software package to other banks and savings and loan associations, first locally and then nationally.

Then out of nowhere, I received an unexpected call. A young, innovative, new company called Electronic Data Systems (EDS) was recruiting talent nationwide. They said they had heard about me from others in St. Louis and wanted to talk to me about coming to work for them. I had never heard of them. To this day, I can't figure out how they got my name. I was flattered and intrigued enough to have an initial interview. I was twenty-seven years old and felt pretty pumped! I agreed to fly to Dallas to learn more. I participated in a couple of interviews, which went well enough for them to fly both Sally and me back to Dallas for more interviews.

They treated Sally and me like royalty. We had dinner and went dancing at a country club with a vice president and the company president, who became a future US presidential candidate, Ross Perot. He danced with Sally; I danced with his wife. It was an incredible night, and we were overwhelmed by their attention. Our interest was piqued!

The next day, we got in a car, and someone from the company drove us around to look for houses. The houses we saw were new, and the landscape seemed flat. The whole day we drove around, and I can't remember seeing a tree. The homes we saw were very nice, but reality began to set in. Sally loved old houses and antiques. The neighborhoods were new; Texas was hot and flat. We'd lived in St. Louis all our lives. It was home, and both of our families were there. Our boys were three and one, and on the flight home, we also considered what it would be like for them growing up so far away from their grandparents. Neither Sally nor I had the experience of knowing our grandparents, and we both felt it was important for the boys. Weighing everything, we made a decision. When EDS called a week later with a job offer, I turned it down.

But my experience with Ross Perot's company got me thinking about my next step after IBM. Maybe I had something more in me that I hadn't yet realized. I decided to approach First National Bank and try to create a spot for myself in their organization, which would ultimately land me in the position of assistant vice president of computers.

As word spread, the demand for the software the team had created grew well beyond what Red Burkhartsmeier, vice president of computers for First National Bank, and the rest of bank management, could have imagined. Many of the regular programming staff in Red's department were struggling to focus on the business of the bank while juggling the business this software had created. Many of the programmers in the computer department were spending the majority of their day on the phone with other banks, either handling sales calls or providing support for the systems the bank had sold. These demands stretched the bank's resources thin, and I saw that the bank was coming to a crossroads. They needed to find a way to complete critical system projects for the entire bank, as well as the demand for design, programming, and customer service for this fledgling technology business that had sprouted up beneath their feet. It was causing them business pains.

After working for the bank for over a year, I realized that I might be able to provide this service to the bank. I knew this system better than anyone at the bank and at IBM. The idea of starting my own company energized me. The new company could handle the sales, support, and maintenance of the software business that was causing a headache for the bank. After considering what that company should look like, I landed on the business model that would launch Financial Data Systems. I planned to acquire the right to sell the software, sharing the proceeds with the bank, and provide support and maintenance to existing and new customers. As the pieces began to form in my mind, I actually thought I could pull it off. I was confident that I could make this idea work. I knew the software and service needs of this application as well as anyone in the industry. I began to think about what I needed to complete the team, and that was a seasoned salesperson.

One of my favorite principles is that "nothing happens until someone sells something."

One evening, Sally and I were relaxing with neighbors on the side porch of their home on Cheyenne Court in Glendale, Missouri. Katie and Alan (Al) Feather had become good friends of ours, and on many pleasant evenings, we'd tuck the boys into bed and visit. Alan was a gifted salesman and had been with Corning Glass for many years. That night I told them about the business plan I'd been working out, and they both were excited about the prospect. I thought Al could be an ideal person to sell the system, and he was interested in joining the effort. Al had the natural ability to sell, but he needed to understand the technical issues before selling the software we'd be working with. So, I sent him to IBM school to learn some things about computer technology, and to see if he had an aptitude. About a week into training, he came back to me and told me he thought what I was doing was great, but it was too far over his head. He decided to stick with his current job, but he became one of the first to invest in Financial Data Systems.

It was a disappointment to lose Al, but my resolve was not shaken. I went to work the next day, and Bill Corrington came to mind. Bill and I had been working together since I had moved to the bank. He'd replaced Bob Fischer, who I'd been partnered with, and we worked well together. We had different personalities, but I knew we had the same dedication to setting and achieving goals. After some careful thought, I decided to approach him and lay out my plan. I scheduled some time with him one afternoon when he was at First National Bank and explained the business model I was building and that I needed somebody to help sell it. I asked him to leave IBM and join me as an equal partner, heading up the sales side of the business.

Bill needed time to think about the proposal. He needed to figure out if he wanted to leave IBM. It was a big decision to leave the security he had and venture out on his own. We talked several times over the course of the month that it took him to make his decision, but he eventually decided the risk was worth it and he joined me as an equal partner at FDS.

With the salesman lined up, I was ready to approach First National Bank with the idea. We wrote a proposal to bring to the bank, Bill giving it his sales spin and me handling the logistics of how the business side of things would work. We had a meeting with my boss, Red Burkhartsmeier, to get his thoughts. They were neutral. He wanted to solve his problem, but he didn't want to lose me. I then went to Red's boss, Jay Wellman, and outlined what Financial Data Systems would do for the bank and how the businesses could work together. Jay had many questions for me, which we took as a good sign. But as the meeting drew to a close, Jay turned to me with his decision. I remember it clearly to this day.

"No! Not just no, but unequivocally NO!" Jay left the room, and I drove home . . . angry.

My idea solved many problems for the bank, and I knew it needed to happen. I couldn't wrap my head around how Jay couldn't see that. I went into what Sally and the boys would come to call my "cave," and I thought carefully for a couple of weeks about how I was going to get around this. One morning it came to me in the shower, a place where I do some of my best thinking. I came out, reinvigorated, and told Sally I had the solution: I needed to go over Jay Wellman's head to the president of First National Bank, and I had to find a connection that would get me to him.

A week later, I was in the office of the bank president Edwin (Ted) S. Jones. I had told his secretary I was an AVP in the data processing group, and I had an issue I needed to discuss directly with Mr. Jones. That got me in the door. Once I was there, I laid everything out for him. My proposal included a revenue-sharing plan that would be quite lucrative for the bank but would require no upfront capital to purchase the rights to the software. I also wanted him to understand the full picture, so in addition to the proposal, I told him about the EDS job opportunity that I had declined earlier when I decided to come to work for First National.

I think Mr. Jones knew I was not long for the bank and that they were faced with losing a valuable resource in short order. He asked me a few questions and then said, "Let me take this under consideration."

After the way I'd left the meeting with Jay Wellman a couple weeks earlier, I took this as a promising sign. The bank had begun missing important deadlines for projects that would further its real business, so I knew there was a demonstrable value in my proposal. I was excited and nervous when I got word that Mr. Jones was on the line calling to speak with me. I picked up the phone and was exhilarated to hear him say the officers had agreed to my proposal, with a few modifications. My new business just took its first step!

Now we needed to raise some funding. I didn't think we needed much to get started, because we were going to have some revenue from the maintenance contracts we were going to take over from the bank. I thought that $25,000 would be plenty. Neither Bill Corrington nor I had much money. I had a young family and $5,000 in my savings account. We both thought we could get by on $800 per month for a year. So, we started to contact people we knew who might have some excess funds to invest. The only ones I knew were the fathers of my high school classmates who seemed to have good jobs and financial comfort. I made a list, which included my dad. Bill did the same. Bill's list contained some classmates from prominent St. Louis families. There were no duplicates in our respective lists. We decided to try to raise $3,000 from at least eight people, with Bill and me each investing $500, which got us to $25,000. We sold 30 percent of the company stock to the investors, and Bill and I split the remaining 70 percent evenly, as founder's stock. Several of the investors became members of our first board of directors. We chose directors based on their expertise that would fill voids in our experience, like personnel and marketing. One of the directors, Walter Metcalfe, was an attorney Bill knew, and he became a lifelong friend of mine. I became president, and Bill was vice president.

Being an entrepreneur takes courage, tenacity, wisdom, and a lot of God's providence, I might add. To step outside the boundaries of the usual way of operating and try something new takes courage. You have to have the tenacity and wisdom to trust yourself and see a good idea through. You have to follow your passion and your energy and worry about your livelihood second. I had been committed to founding this business. I stepped out on my own from a deep conviction this was the right thing to do and was the direction in which my career path was taking me.

My journey to becoming an entrepreneur had a significant impact on my life and the way I ran my businesses. I learned lessons by working through disappointments, and I was able to open the doors at Financial Data Systems on October 23, 1968. I gained life principles in trusting my instincts with a willingness to take a risk.

Chapter 3
COMPETING

It was my sophomore year at Webster Groves High School, and the varsity baseball team was winning one of the last games of the season by a comfortable margin. I was riding the bench, much as I had been the entire season, when Coach Froebel Gaines, whom we called "Froggy" behind his back, yelled over his shoulder, "Canfield, go bat for James." Charley James was a senior at Webster, and we all knew he and another standout athlete, Hank Kuhlmann, had college and possible pro careers ahead of them.

As a sophomore on the same roster with Charlie and Hank, I was firmly stuck in the bottom of the roster. But that day Coach Gaines didn't have much to lose, so he took a chance and put me in for James. I made my way up to the plate and took my position. I was nervous, but on the first pitch, I singled to the outfield, right between the third baseman and shortstop. It was the first, and only, time the coach called my name that year, but for that season, I batted 1.000. That was my memorable debut in varsity sports.

Like many of my high school friends, I played the big three sports: football, basketball, and baseball. I love sports and competition, my favorite being basketball. Whether competing, spectating, or coaching my boys, I am fascinated by all aspects of athletics. It is through sports that I learned teamwork, perseverance in the face of failure, discipline, and sportsmanship. These character principles became foundational in my business life. In fact, I was attracted to a girl in junior high because of sports. I later married her.

Sally and I were what you'd consider typical high school kids in the 1950s. We grew up in the upper-middle class, midwestern suburb of Webster Groves, Missouri. Both of us came from traditional families. My mom was college educated and stayed well-read throughout her life, but her primary job was to stay at home and take care of my brother and me, volunteering at local civic organizations and nonprofits in her spare time.

Dad was a typical man's man. He went to work Monday through Friday at Sporlan Valve, but often, at day's end, he would head to the Tulip Bar to pull up a stool, have a beer, and talk with some friends. He always made it home in time to take his seat at the dinner table, and he made time on the weekends for hunting, fishing, and camping. I never actually related to his pull toward the outdoors, but we could pass hours talking about business and science.

My generation was nicknamed the "Silent Generation" because it was common thinking among parents of the time that children were expected to be obedient. Households were parent-controlled, and children did not challenge that authority. The Depression and World War II shaped our parents' lives. Times were difficult and there were no luxuries. Money was tight, and we economized in every area of life. I remember helping Mom put green stamps in booklets she could redeem for two dollars. I popped the inserted yellow capsule and squeezed bags of white oleo until the oleo turned yellow, so it looked like butter.

Our generation was known for working hard and playing by the rules. Our lives were not driven by technology, and when Sally and I talked on the phone at night, we made our calls on a corded, rotary dial telephone that was in either the dining room or the living room. If our parents were waiting for an important phone call, we stayed off the phone, so we didn't tie up the line. We listened to radio shows like *The Lone Ranger*, *The Shadow*, and *Bobby Benson and the B-Bar-B Riders*. When I was ten years old, I was the first kid in my class to get a seven-inch TV. We invited the entire fourth grade class over to our house to watch Harry Truman's inaugural address of 1949. With this new TV, there was no color. We had one channel during the day, and test patterns at night. My favorite show was *Howdy Doody*, with Buffalo Bob and Clarabelle, the clown. To fill some of our evenings, we had "sock hops" in a crepe paper–decorated school gym, shared the family car, and frequented White Castle after basketball games where I put away twelve "belly bomber burgers," and Sally had six!

The 1950s in Webster Groves were generally quiet and embraced traditional values. Our group of friends had a reputation for being a smart, clean-cut group. Good grades were important to us, and when we weren't studying, we'd play pick-up games in our backyards or empty fields, catch a movie at the Ozark Theater, or play the occasional poker or bridge game. We didn't smoke or drink, and it was an act of defiance if we stayed out long after our curfew.

Sally and I met in homeroom on the first day of seventh grade. We'd made the leap from grade school classes of 30 to high school with an incoming class of 325. There was no junior high. Grades seven through twelve were all together. As new seventh graders, we felt like little fish in an ocean—forget the pond. In homeroom, we went around and introduced ourselves the first day, and that was when I officially met Sally Martin. Sally and I ran in the same circles and had mutual friends, so we naturally got to know each other. We had a shared love of music—Sally was a gifted pianist, and I sang tenor in the school choir—but it was our mutual love of baseball that really kindled our friendship in those early days of high school. This girl who had all the Cardinals' batting averages memorized fascinated me. I didn't stand a chance when Sally showed me her scrapbook devoted to Stan Musial.

In the eighth grade, everyone began testing out boy-girl relationships. Notes started flying around the classroom when the teacher's back was turned, many of them listing crushes in numerical order, and the boys began teasing their favorite girls as they passed them in the hallway. It has always been my fashion to go for the more direct approach, though, and I asked my favorite Cardinals fan to dance with me at a cotillion dance. She said yes. The more Sally and I got to know each other, the more our friendship grew.

By our sophomore year of high school, Sally and I started dating exclusively. Back then, dating meant talking on the phone every night, walking to class together and occasionally sitting next to each other. Sally and I met friends for double dates and enjoyed going to the movies together. Sally's high school sorority hosted dances, and Sally was always my date. Silver ID bracelets became popular, and everyone was wearing them. It was the tradition that when you started "going steady" with a girl, you would exchange ID bracelets with her. And, as the tradition went, you knew you were being dumped when you got yours back.

When Sally and I exchanged bracelets, making it official, I came home that afternoon to quite a lecture from Mom. No matter how fond she was of Sally, she did not like me giving her my bracelet. I didn't want to lose Sally by breaking tradition, so every morning before school, I met Sally at her locker to exchange bracelets. She would wear it during the day, and we'd make sure we exchanged it back before I went home in the afternoon. Sally and I were officially "going together" in the eyes of our Webster friends all day, but Mom was none the wiser each evening.

Sally came to many of my games and said she thought it was extra special to be dating a basketball player. I played various sports year-round but was particularly adept at basketball. During one basketball season, we began a postgame ritual that has carried on through our marriage. And for better or worse, we handed it down to our granddaughter, Becky. When the final buzzer sounded, I headed back to the locker room with the team, and Sally waited outside with the other girls who were dating players. Sally and I then headed to the previously mentioned White Castle experience.

Basketball was something of a family legacy. My dad was an outstanding player, and a letterman for the basketball team at Miami University in Oxford, Ohio. Dad taught me to play on a court he built in our backyard. My friends and I practiced there after school on a regular basis. As I got older, the games with my dad got fewer, and my friends and I would be playing in the backyard when Dad would come home from the Tulip Bar with slurred speech and a bad disposition, then fall asleep on the couch. It was part of his routine that troubled me more as I got older. I didn't like it, especially when my friends were around. One afternoon we were working on a project together in the backyard. I gathered my courage and took a deep breath, turned to my dad and said, "Dad, I'm going to start telling you when I plan to bring friends to the house. And on those days, I would appreciate it if you wouldn't drink."

I had a tremendous amount of respect for my dad, and I'd never confronted an adult before—let alone one of my parents. I steeled myself for his response. It was a show of how much character he had when he regarded me thoughtfully for a moment and agreed to it. We made a deal that I would tell him a day ahead of time when I was planning to have friends over, and he would skip the Tulip Bar. As difficult as that conversation was, I sensed that he respected and appreciated the way I handled talking to him. Our relationship remained close, and he stuck to our agreement through my senior year when, as a graduation present, he stopped drinking and joined Alcoholics Anonymous (AA). Dad stayed sober for the remainder of his life, and I was really touched when, at his funeral, I heard story after story about people whom he had helped to sobriety, either as a sponsor in AA or through his time as "Mr. X" on KMOX radio. This was a program where an unnamed member of AA posed as "Mr. X" and answered questions called in by listeners.

I played basketball throughout high school, but, unlike Dad, I didn't play more than recreationally after I moved on to Purdue University. My sons, Jim and Tom, were both as enthusiastic about sports as I had been growing up, and our family was always playing and competing against each other at home. One of our special father/son times was to attend NCAA Final Four basketball tournament games. Each year, before the tournament started, I would accumulate tickets I had won in the annual ticket lottery. These were usually for seats at the top of the stadium. We would get to the tournament site a day early and start trying to upgrade our seat locations by trading with fans and scalpers. In addition to the cash that I also took, we would offer several of our nosebleed tickets for one better ticket. We generally had decent seats for the first two games on Saturday by this trading technique. After each of the first two games, we would negotiate with fans of the losing teams to buy their tickets for the final game on Monday. Because their teams would not be playing, they were usually willing to get some money back. This is where the cash really came in handy. Using these tickets, we spent Sunday trading up to prime seats for the final game.

Sally and I had access to Cardinals tickets since the boys were little, so we spent many summer weekends at Busch Stadium cheering on baseball legends. One of my contractual "perks" from the sale of TALX to Equifax was access to season box seats owned by TALX.

Sally isn't one to just sit on the sidelines and be a spectator, though. She'd noticed my mom was always off to the side, deep in

COMPETING

a book, while the rest of my family was playing touch football or cards, and that just wasn't in her nature. In fact, Sally has always been athletic and took pride in being chosen before some of the boys in grade school softball games. Sally was just as competitive on the slopes of Snowmass or on the tennis court as the rest of us. I enjoyed tennis, as well, so we put in a tennis court in our backyard for the whole family to enjoy, but she and I enjoyed it the most, competing in mixed doubles together.

We supported the boys' athletics as much as possible. Sally cheered them on from the sidelines, and I would leave work and head straight to the field for baseball practice to coach. I rolled the legs of my suit pants up and coached from the sidelines before grabbing dinner and heading back to the office to squeeze in a few more hours of work. Being a part of the boys' sports gave me the opportunity to take a break from whatever problem was consuming me at the time, and instead focus on the boys. So basketball, baseball, football, hockey, skiing, and tennis were more than casual pursuits to us. They were important threads in my relationship with Sally and the boys.

It was ultimately Jim and Tom's love of sports that led to a renewed focus and intensity of faith in our lives. Sally was at the pool at Westborough Country Club with the boys one hot afternoon, talking to Mary Grace Moore, when the club's swim team came up. Most of the members' children were on the team, including our boys, so Sally asked why none of

Moore's five kids had joined. Mary Grace told her, "My kids go to a camp in the summertime. It is three and a half weeks long, and we feel it is better for them than the swim team."

Sally had always been impressed with the character and politeness she'd seen in Mary Grace's children, so her curiosity was aroused. Mary Grace went on to tell her that the camp, Kamp Kanakuk, was the reason why they were such great kids. She said counselors talked about Jesus, because the camp had a spiritual aspect. I like to call it the "Jocks and Jesus Kamp" because Kanakuk was a Christian sports camp and many of the counselors were varsity college athletes, as well as committed Christians.

Sally was raised going to church with her family. My parents thought it important that I went, but they did not go. I was dropped off for and picked up from Sunday school. One disturbing memory was being an acolyte for the worship service. While I was serving in that capacity, the Episcopal priest handed me the wine chalice with instructions to drink the unfinished wine. The whole experience so upset me at age twelve that I never returned to that church. Years later, Sally and I got involved in an active youth group at Webster Presbyterian Church. It was a very positive experience and erased some of the painful memories of my younger years.

We raised the boys with a sense that attending church was important to our family. Sally took the kids to church

COMPETING

every Sunday, and I joined them on the days when I wasn't working. We prayed a rote prayer at dinner. We thought we were Christians but really were not. We did not understand what that meant until later. Everything Mary Grace told Sally about Kanakuk impressed her. She wanted to know more. Before leaving the pool for the day, Sally asked to be invited to the recruiting presentation the camp was planning to hold in St. Louis the following winter.

When the time came, Sally took Jim with her to the Kamp movies, plopped him in the front row, and settled in to find out more about Kamp Kanakuk. She and Jim came back talking nonstop about kids on ropes courses, tennis courts, water-skiing boats, jumping on the "Blob" and playing football and baseball. Sally thought it looked fun, even for an adult. She was sold, and so was Jim. That summer we put Jim, our eleven-year-old son, on a bus to spend three and a half weeks at camp in the Branson, Missouri, countryside. All parents were asked to come down and spend the final two days of the session to watch competitions and experience the Kamp with the kids.

After three weeks, we headed down to Kamp for a few days and to bring Jim home. Sally observed with fascination how the counselors worked with the kids, being positive and encouraging them until they had completed a race or other competition.

We both watched a counselor jump in the water during a swim meet to cheer on a boy who wanted to quit. The counselor encouraged him to the finish line, where all the parents who were watching the meet cheered for this child, who persevered to the end. Parents cheered more for the reluctant finisher than they did for the winner of the race. We watched counselors guide children through conflict resolution with grace and humility. That evening we went to vespers. This was no ordinary camp. Kids were being taught life values and character like we had never seen before. Sally came home moved and challenged.

I wasn't as struck by the aura of the experience as she was, but we continued to send Jim each summer, and then Tom, once he was old enough. I had to admit when they returned they were different kids . . . for about six weeks. They didn't fight and were extraordinarily polite, but that would all disintegrate once they got back to school. It wasn't just the kids; Sally noticed she also struggled to reacclimatize after living the experience at Kanakuk for only a few days.

After a few years of this cycle, Sally began to question why such a unique lifestyle only existed in the confines of the camp. Her questions and our experiences at that summer sports camp led her on a faith journey that was life changing.

Since Sally grew up going to church, her curiosity about Christianity became more intense and she joined Bible Study Fellowship. In that organization, she began to grow in her understanding of the Bible and made a commitment to Jesus

COMPETING

Christ. On many occasions, I remember her coming home quite excited, wanting to share with me the new things she was learning about her faith, things we'd never talked about before.

I enjoyed seeing her so enthusiastic, but I didn't have the same interest level as she did. I was tolerant but told her, "I think that's perfect for you, honey, but it's not for me." She was wise enough not to push too hard. She let me grow on my own.

Chapter 4
A DECISION THAT CHANGED EVERYTHING

Over the next months, we began to socialize with couples Sally knew from the Bible Study Fellowship, and we began to form new friendships. Sally's closest friend was Myrna Anderson, whose husband, Steve, worked at what is now called KPMG, a national accounting firm with offices in St. Louis. We spent a lot of time together, and eventually, I ended up in an eight-week study group with them and five other couples. I agreed to attend, thinking it would be a great opportunity for more social interaction. I had never heard of the book we were going to read, Josh McDowell's *Evidence That Demands a Verdict*.

When I began the study, I realized I didn't have a full understanding of Jesus Christ. I didn't have a clear picture of his unique claims. I knew he was a good person, but that knowledge didn't make any demands on me, morally or spiritually. I was a good man already, certainly a responsible father, husband, and businessman. Wasn't that good enough?

I had never systematically examined his claims. I began to discover what he taught specifically about his person and purpose in coming to earth, the prophecies he fulfilled, the historical context and sources that verified and established his existence, and that he was a deity come in the flesh. My eyes were opened during each week as we met, but it was in the seventh week, reading the chapter "Trilemma—Liar, Lunatic, or Lord?" that my defenses finally broke down. Logic appeals to me, and the arguments put forth in that chapter made me think that I had to get off the fence and either accept or reject his claims. The section laid out a logical diagram, a flow chart that posed a series of questions that led me to specific conclusions: If Christ was a liar, then I could dismiss him. That was a path I could take, but I couldn't do it. There was too much evidence that he wasn't lying. And I had no reason to believe he was engaged in lunacy. That only left the third alternative, that Christ was who he said he was—Lord and Savior. I realized that the particular truth that Jesus is the Son of God demanded a response from me.

After that evening's discussion, I knew I had to decide what I believed about Jesus Christ. I did go home and pray a sinner's prayer in the privacy of my own room. I didn't have a heaven-opening experience, but my life definitely began to change, at least in my thinking, and in how I approached my relationships, both personal and professional.

In the past, I had not spent any time reading the Bible. It was new and refreshing to me. I followed my wife's example: I joined the men's group of the Bible Study Fellowship. Over the next few years, I studied Romans, Genesis, the Gospel of John, and a few of the Minor Prophets. There were many exciting discoveries, and one in particular stands out: that God chose me. He knew me before the foundations of the world, elected me to sonship. He had chosen me when I was in college, when I got married, and for the first fifteen years of my business career, while I did things my own way. During all that time he protected me and put up with me. Among all the things I was learning, I was struck by his goodness. All this time, I'd been taken care of, protected, kept for that moment when I would receive the truth. I hadn't acknowledged any of his kindness toward me.

Slowly, my life began taking on new dimensions. I felt exhilarated to get into the swing of things and understand how much God had been present yet unknown to me. A new excitement pervaded my thinking.

A little later, I attended a seminar given by Larry Burkett. He called the program Business by the Book. He took us through his book of the same title, teaching us "a radical new approach to business management." He touched on everything a person needs to deal with in running a business based on Christian principles: business bondage, personal lifestyle goals, biblical business goals, and much more. By the time I was done with that seminar, I had an entirely new way of looking at my business operations, at how I had treated people, and most of all, what God expected of me.

What impressed me about Burkett was how he related each of his ideas to specific Bible passages and scriptures, and how he elucidated basic biblical principles.

Over time, I developed a new model of life in my mind, one vastly different from the one I'd operated by up to that moment. I began to notice that when I talked to an employee or when I needed to do a little counseling, reprimanding, or even giving a raise, there was a difference in the way I integrated all of the biblical knowledge I'd been learning. The Bible is clear that Christians need to treat people with great respect. I was far from perfect in all my dealings, but I did have a new realization of how important it was to treat people with kindness and grace, something new to my thinking. Not only did I have a new set of principles, but I also had the sense that the Holy Spirit was within me now, giving me the right perspective.

Part of my new sensibility toward people was my overwhelming thankfulness to God for how patient and forgiving he'd been toward me. God had granted me abundant grace, keeping me safe in my ignorance until the moment when I would understand his truth and love and receive it. Extending that same grace to others became one of my most passionate principles: he extended grace toward me so that in turn, I could extend grace to those around me. Right beside all the other biblical principles of financial management that I brought into my business, I endeavored to incorporate a sense of freedom to fail, company-wide. This created such a positive workplace environment that allowed new ideas to flourish in ways that were beyond my expectations. This culture, which I will discuss more fully later, became one of the critical components to our spectacular success in growing a floundering company into a billion-dollar enterprise in twelve years.

Chapter 5
THE MAIN THING

Sally and I were married in a candlelit ceremony at Webster Groves Christian Church on September 2, 1961. The ceremony was held three months after we graduated, me from Purdue with my degree in electrical engineering and Sally from Miami of Ohio with a degree in English and education. Everything about the ceremony and the reception that followed at Algonquin Golf Club was stunning, especially Sally. Our parents were happy for us, and my parents loved Sally, but they'd asked me to wait until I'd finished graduate school before we got married. We didn't want to wait. We were already engaged before we left college, and I'd already started my MBA program at Washington University in St. Louis a couple months prior, so I didn't see the point in waiting. But a result of that decision was that my parents told us Sally and I were on our own when it came to paying for college and housing, which was fine with us. We knew we could manage. Sally already had a job teaching eighth grade English at East Ladue Junior High. We would manage on her $4,600 annual salary, and I would earn extra money folding and stuffing bulb clamps, nuts, and bolts in an envelope for Sporlan Valve. And we did!

We moved into an apartment in Richmond Heights, not far from campus and not far from East Ladue. Getting my master's in business administration was the right decision since I had no desire to be an electrical engineer. The engineering curriculum was a great foundation, teaching me to think logically in math and science, which I loved. The business degree paired well with the engineering for my career.

I was a STEM guy before anyone decided to make it an acronym. When it came time to declare a major at Purdue, I went with chemical engineering first. In high school, I had earned an A and a B in chemistry class. The A was for me, and the B was for Sally, who, as a future English major, needed tutoring. So, chemical engineering seemed a safe route for me. Freshman year of undergrad rolled around, and I found out rather quickly I didn't like labs. I failed my first chemistry class partially due to Sigma Chi pledge training, which took up most of my free time. But it was also because I didn't like the labs. I took chemistry again in summer school and passed, but I made the switch to electrical engineering and never looked back.

My engineering education at Purdue gave me outstanding problem-solving skills. Even as a young boy, I had an innate drive to solve problems. My mom and I shared that passion. My brother Tom likes to tell the story about working on a logic puzzle for a day and a half. Tom ran in to show her he'd finally solved it, beaming with pride. He thought it would stump her as it did him, but it only took her eight minutes to solve. Not that Tom, a future Harvard MBA graduate, was slow. My mom was just that smart.

Back to my dislike of labs, in my senior year when I interviewed for electrical engineering jobs, I was often toured through some form of a lab. I like to be with people, and for me, those labs represented isolation. If I was going to enter the business world, I needed to learn as much about business, economics, and people as I could. That motivated me to enroll in the MBA program at Washington University in St. Louis, where I completed my degree in thirteen months. When I walked out of Washington University with my diploma in hand, I felt like I had a well-rounded education that prepared me for the technology industry. I was ready to enter the workforce. My breadth of thinking, and my ability to interact with people—the same personality trait that didn't allow me to be stuck in a lab—are what helped me secure my first job out of college at International Business Machines, better known as IBM.

IBM is one of the longest-operating computer companies in the world, and when I joined it in September of 1962, personal computing was in its infancy, and the internet was embryonic. In 1911, when the company was formed, IBM sold business machines such as timekeeping equipment, scales, coffee grinders, and meat slicers. They also sold punch-card equipment, which eventually evolved into computer systems. Their primary focus, though, was helping businesses work smarter. What made IBM stand out, and what I think contributed to its longevity, was the constant focus on industry trends.

I also interviewed with Southwestern Bell and Bell Labs, which, along with IBM, were responsible for some of the best scientific research in the country at the time. IBM had a sales office in St. Louis, and Southwestern Bell (SBC) was also headquartered in St. Louis. Dad had worked for Southwestern Bell for some years as an estimator on the business side. He made a connection for me. I went to their offices and sat down with a recruiter. We talked about my background and education, goals, and accomplishments. It was standard for a job interview, and things were going well. The conversation was promising, but then the interviewer pulled out a massive, three-ring binder, put it on the table in front of me, and opened to the first page. He flipped through page after page, and the corporate ladder reached higher and higher. My eyes couldn't help but glaze over as I thought about whether I ever stood a chance of going anywhere with their company.

I got back into my car, a little overwhelmed by their structure and disappointed in what I saw in that binder. As

I drove home, I realized working for SBC meant the slow path to management, and, in turn, a career spent executing the visions of those in the chart above me. I knew I wanted to lead a team and be involved in innovating new technologies. I couldn't imagine how a corporate ladder that reached ad infinitum would give me a chance to innovate, or how anyone in that chart could effect real change.

From the start of the recruiting process, I knew IBM was different. Before I sat down for a face-to-face interview, I completed a series of tests. The tests I took were unlike any others I'd seen. The questions they asked challenged my logic and asked about my view of the world. IBM was looking for people who could not only create and install computer systems, but for those they could trust to represent the company inside their customers' walls. They had to have the knowledge to do the job and possess the personality to be the face of the company. The recruiters said my results showed a unique combination of technical and business skills and a good fit for a systems engineer position. I would work closely with the sales team and clients to build and implement IBM systems to solve specific problems with their technology. I accepted the position, and on September 11, 1962, I started my first IBM sales training class in downtown St. Louis, with an annual salary of $7,200. Together, Sally and I were making over $11,000 per year! We thought we were set for life!

Only a few colleges and universities offered degrees in computer science at that time. So companies like IBM had to train their own, and IBM's training program was outstanding. We went through a series of classes and learned the 1401/1440 computer system and "Autocoder," a programming language. Our training group attended an eight-week class and then went into the field for hands-on experience, alternating the two throughout the course of our twenty-month training. I took a leave of absence for six months to fulfill my military obligation at the end of the first training class, missing a field assignment. After the second class, my first field assignment had me working with accounting machines and punch cards, which was probably where I picked up the habit of carrying cards around in my pocket. Eventually, technology changed, and those punch cards were replaced with internal processors in the computers and three-by-five index cards in my pocket.

In my early days with IBM, planning and building computer systems, I learned the number one business principle that has driven almost every business decision I've made:

Solve problems with technology. Don't sell technology; sell solutions to someone's problem using technology. Be the aspirin for their business headache.

My time at IBM launched me headlong into the world of computers and lit the sign I tell people is emblazoned in my mind, flashing the message, "Solve problems using technology."

I went on to either found or purchase several computer-related companies, all based around the idea of solving someone's problem with technology.

As I went on to build or reshape those companies, the image of that three-ring binder on the table in the Southwestern Bell recruiter's office stayed with me. I will always remember how it had stood out to me that the hierarchy seemed like the antithesis of innovation. When I worked to solve problems with technology, I also tried to keep the company hierarchy relatively flat. I made sure people could see the top management, could question the status quo, could think differently, and felt comfortable enough to express their opinions. That structure was imperative to supporting an atmosphere of innovation at both Financial Data Systems and TALX. It was something that everyone who worked with the company felt just as strongly about as I did.

Chapter 6
PUTTING THE TEAM TOGETHER

The St. Louis Cardinals are a world-class baseball organization, and I'm not just saying that out of blind loyalty. Sally and I have sat behind the dugout and watched the Cardinals celebrate thirteen division titles, eight National League pennants, and three World Series titles, as of the writing of this book. As Busch Stadiums II and III were filled with confetti, fireworks, and the deafening roar of the best fans in baseball, the team celebrated each of those wins with a sense of Midwestern humility and gratitude.

On the flip side, we also sat in the same seats and watched the team handle their fair share of losing bids for championship titles and pennant races with grace and dignity—suffice it to say the 1970s and the 1990s weren't good decades for the team for reasons that could fill a whole different book.

In recent decades, however, there has been something special about the management, coaches, and players. Recently, it has been called the "Cardinal Way," and speculation is that the "Way" made the team work. It is more than a marketing slogan or throwaway catchphrase. There is tested reasoning behind why the team has such a solid lineup and is able to keep it that way with a limited payroll. It starts with a scouting practice that balances a player's numbers and natural ability and ends with the world-class farm league the team relies on to develop well-rounded players. Taken together, the Cardinals organization procures and nurtures talented players differently than most other teams in Major League Baseball. Cardinals management has developed a world-class organization that consistently finishes on top—on the field and off. Their recruiting and management practices are enviable, and many business leaders could take a note or two from the Cardinals' playbook. Could I find something in their approach that I could adapt to my business?

It was more by trial and error than observation from the stands that I stumbled upon a similar combination of metrics and employee development. It started with the increasing demand for services at FDS. The business pressures that stretched the boundaries of First National Bank and birthed FDS continued, as word spread among the banking institutions. In the fall of 1968, when FDS began, Bill Corrington was in charge of sales, I handled the customer and technical sides, and Maxine Harvey was our girl Friday. We had set up a small office in the Boatmen's Bank Building. It was furnished with orange crates and used furniture, but we chose an address that suggested substance. Soon, Tom Boswell left First National Bank and joined us to handle the customer maintenance calls. Because we needed more administrative work, we hired Kathy McDonald, our neighbor and the boys' babysitter. It was a slim beginning!

By the fall of 1969, we had prospered, growing to a full-fledged company with ten employees and proper desks, filing cabinets, and chairs. We then moved to offices on Chippewa in south St. Louis City.

As we grew, FDS had a couple of hires who, for one reason or another, weren't a good fit. So we had to let some go and move others to different jobs. I learned quickly that letting an employee go is hard for everyone. It is no fun. I also learned that I couldn't tell much about a person's ability or personality with just a personal interview. We needed to find a better way to hire. I remembered the testing I went through with IBM and decided to add that facet to our hiring process.

Myers-Briggs says I am an INTJ—an introverted, intuitive, thinking, and judging person. This is a personality type (5 percent of the population) that most descriptions call "The Scientist" or "The Entrepreneur." Perhaps that is where I get my instinct for assessing people and seeing raw potential, but that is more of an art than a science. I wanted to find people who had positive energy, passion, the ability to energize, and who could make and execute on tough calls. We also needed to balance personality, technical ability, and fit within the organization.

At the time, pre-employment testing was new, but IBM and the NFL gave me some examples that proved extremely valuable. I began using the Wonderlic test for aptitude that the NFL was using, and the personality profile test for personality traits and ability that IBM was using at the time.

I gradually learned how to interpret these tests and created a profile that helped find good people who might meet our needs. Eventually, I had the tests administered *before* any interviews occurred with an individual. The testing would screen out applicants who were not qualified before we invested time in getting to know them. Employee testing, and the empirical data it produced, appealed to my senses of logic and order, and it became a staple of employment screening at every business I worked with from FDS forward.

This method worked. The employees at Financial Data Systems, and later at TALX, were some of the hardest-working, most devoted, and technically sound individuals I have had the pleasure of doing business with. We had pulled together a group of sharp people—individuals who were creative, problem solvers, and free thinkers.

Another critical component of hiring new employees was getting a sense of their character. One way of discerning character was "gene pool" hires. They were an important part of the talent we recruited at FDS and TALX. There is something to be said for hiring people whose parents you've known for a long time. There were at least ten others whose parents I knew, and whose values I understood, who passed through the hiring process with high marks. My son Jim, who flew jets for the US Navy off aircraft carriers, received no special advantages in the hiring process. He was expected to meet the same qualifications as other "gene pool" hires. I asked him to commit to five years at TALX, since his ten years of Navy experience had set him behind his peers in the private technology sector. He worked hard, earning the respect of those he worked with, despite having a dad who was the CEO. Jim was at TALX for fifteen years before moving to Seattle to pursue other interests.

Hiring people that other employees knew and recommended was also a way of understanding character. Additionally, this emphasized another one of my business mantras:

People like to work with people they like, and customers will buy more from people they like.

Robert Bell was an example of a star at TALX who came out of left field. Robert was a youth pastor, and his wife, Amy, was in Sally's Bible Study Fellowship leadership class. The two were talking one day, and she described to Sally Robert's situation. He wanted to move from ministry to the business world. I met him, liked him, and invited him to come to TALX. He went through the hiring process at TALX, taking a couple of tests, and going through a chain of interviews. When Robert got to my office, we chatted for a while, and, as I did with everyone who made it that far in the process, I said, "Tell me who you are."

It's a big question that requires a thoughtful response. By the time a candidate entered the CEO's office, they were close to the end of the interview process. My technique of interviewing caused people to think and answer honestly. It could be nerve-wracking, and you could see hints of apprehension surfacing in people as they answered. With no structure, outline, or suggestion as to what I was listening for, prospects would go in a couple of different directions with their answers. Some focused on their work, others would begin talking about their families. Naturally, and likely because they were in a job interview, some would jump straight to accomplishments. I would listen politely and then say, "That's great, you have told me *what* you are, but tell me *who* you are." I was more interested in hearing about families and hobbies, though. I wanted to understand the whole person. As Robert and I talked, it was evident he was bright, and his personality was a good fit for TALX. I spoke with everyone who had interviewed him and looked at his test results. They told me the same thing. We offered Robert a position with TALX, and he worked in sales until long after I retired.

Testing continued to prove its value repeatedly in every organization where I used it. I found that after fine-tuning the recruiting process, in conjunction with interviews and other soft evaluations, tests were an invaluable tool for creating an efficient, successful organization filled with folks who enjoyed working there. That wasn't just my personal belief, either. TALX was voted one of the "Best Places to Work" by local and national publications several times, based on responses from employees. Our turnover rate was always much lower than that of other technology companies.

I'm acutely aware that you can have a fantastic product and revolutionize your industry, but it is the people who create the goods and services, who build relationships that create sales, and who serve our customers with love and dignity. These are the ones who make the difference. If you don't have the right people in place to support and sell, you don't have much to build upon. My advice to everyone is this:

In business and in life, always find ways to surround yourself with the best people you can find.

Chapter 7
MUSIC IN MY SOUL

In the spring of sixth grade, I got on a bus with sixth graders from several elementary schools in the Webster Groves and Rock Hill area. These were students who would be attending Webster Groves High School the following fall. They were invited to an undeveloped corner of St. Louis County where Camp Wyman sat, in Wildwood, Missouri. It was an exciting week for all of us, making friends with kids we would know for the next six years. For many, it was the first time they had been away from home for a week.

One afternoon, about midway through the camp, I was in the dining hall with some friends of mine. We were just messing around and talking while the rest of our future classmates made their way into the hall for lunch. I don't remember the details, but I know my Hudson School music teacher pulled me aside and asked me to sing to all those sixth graders at lunch. I must have said yes, because I remember her silencing the room as I climbed onto a table to sing. I have no memory of what I sang, but I do know that my singing left a lasting impression on a sixth-grade girl from Goodall School by the name of Sally Martin. What I didn't know then is that ten years later, music would again play a major role in our relationship, in the form of Mendelssohn's "Wedding March."

The Bill Canfield home was a musical one, and hardly a day went by without at least a phrase or two in tune from a Broadway show finding their way into a conversation or our dinner table. I never shied away from a chance to break into song, because a few bars could dispel the tension in the room, at home or in the office. Music lifts the spirits, touches the soul, and moves the heart. And who couldn't use a little more levity in their lives? It was a fantastic way to lessen the tension that was hanging in a conference room.

I credit Rogers and Hammerstein, Lerner and Loewe, and Gershwin, for playing a part in getting a handful of TALX employees and me out of lower Manhattan safely following the terrorist attacks on September 11, 2001. Like many people who were in New York that day, I have a vivid memory of that Tuesday morning. The several other TALX employees and I had stayed in a variety of hotels, including the Marriott World Trade Center Hotel, because we were there for different purposes. A few of us were there to call on investors; others were there to make sales calls. I was there to meet with some investment bankers. We had a few investor meetings and sales calls scheduled that morning at offices throughout lower Manhattan, including the World Trade Center Towers. Two of our team members were already at LaGuardia, waiting to board a plane to return home. When I left my hotel at Fifth Avenue and Sixty-First Street for my meeting that morning on Thirty-Fourth Street, I saw the smoke and didn't know what it was until I got to my meeting, which was cancelled because of the attack. The city was in crisis, and I was unable to find a cab, so I walked the twenty-seven blocks back to the Pierre Hotel. Naturally, my concern was for the people who were at the World Trade Center when the towers were struck, and in communicating with home.

Thankfully, everyone who worked for TALX got out safely, but we were scattered across the city for a couple of days. One employee had to walk across the Brooklyn Bridge in bare feet because she got locked out of her room. Another boarded a ferry and went to New Jersey.

It was impossible to make a call into or out of New York City for hours after the attacks, but our team finally connected via cell phone. We were faced with a problem. We couldn't fly home, because all air traffic was grounded indefinitely, and mass transit was at a crippling halt. I felt responsible for getting everyone out of the city, so I had to come up with a solution. It occurred to me that Newark Airport would probably have rental cars available and not much demand, because the airport was closed for flights. Taxis and car rentals were at a premium if you could find them, but I hailed a cab and paid $200 to a cabbie to drive me across the George Washington Bridge before the bridge was closed, and to our rendezvous point. We all made it to the airport and rented a van. We traveled for two days to get to St. Louis, singing Broadway songs all the way across the country.

To this day, I become emotional when I read or see something that depicts the events of that day. I am still impacted by it and those families who lost loved ones. In the days and months that followed 9/11, the nation's mood was somber. Each one of us in those cars was shaken by the proximity and weight of what we'd experienced. The songs didn't make light of the situation or diminish the impact it had on us, but it made those two days on the road, racing home to our families, more bearable.

New York is a special place for Sally and me because it was where we went on our first trip. We were unable to take a honeymoon because Sally began teaching the week after our wedding, so we went to New York at Christmastime for five days. We wanted to see something on Broadway, and we wanted to see something new that looked like it was going to be a hit. We picked a winner, ending up with tickets to *How to Succeed in Business Without Really Trying*, during its original Broadway run. When they launched a Broadway revival to mark the show's fiftieth anniversary, we were in New York again, but this time with our granddaughter, Becky, for her high school graduation present. She was tickled to see the role of Robert Morse played by Daniel Radcliffe—better known to everyone outside of theater circles as Harry Potter. The music of Broadway delighted all of us.

Sally was a gifted piano player, and I can still vividly recall being in awe of her talent while watching her at her high school recital performance of Grieg's Piano Concerto. My musical career was brief. I dabbled with the trombone when the school required us to play an instrument in the fourth grade, giving it up very willingly in favor of football in eighth grade. I tried to learn guitar several times, and failed rather spectacularly, before attempting the ukulele. I eventually made peace with the fact that my musical talents were firmly of the singing variety.

When I was very young, I used to spend hours sitting on the floor, listening to music from a record player and trying to memorize the words. My first real singing experience was in high school choir under the direction of Ms. Esther Replogle. She was and remains a legend to most students who attended Webster Groves High School in the '50s and '60s. The experience in her classroom and choir influenced many. She had a strong personality and was a tough disciplinarian. Some of the parents weren't fond of her style because she used emotional tactics to control students. However, she was persuasive and effective in pulling quality performances out of students.

"Miss Rep" was a legend in Webster Groves. Her depiction of Christmas vespers representing the nativity of Christ was a sacred and worshipful experience. No public school could do that today.

When most people sing, they pick up the melody because it's the easiest to hear, and not many people sing first tenor because it's too high. However, I always pick up the harmony and am one of those rare first tenors. As a result, I was one of Miss Rep's favorites. Because she was so well respected by students, she recruited to her choir top-notch kids, and it was considered a privilege to belong.

The choir was the place to be, and to get there, you had to audition with a solo. Sally accompanied me on the piano. When I sang "Lucky Old Sun," that secured my spot in the Beginning Choir my sophomore year. As a junior and senior, I was in the Acapella Choir.

Our senior year Sally and I were both in the choir, and she claims admission only because she was my girlfriend, but she has a good singing voice. Miss Rep promoted caroling groups at Christmas each year, encouraging her choir members to form groups and carol in our community. The tradition stuck, and for forty years after we were married, Sally and I would host friends each Christmas, caroling through Kirkwood, me with my pitch pipe, and someone else with the collection can.

Though our caroling party eventually dwindled, singing, especially at Christmastime, did not. Because of my love of singing, each year at TALX, we made a big deal out of the Christmas party. My administrative assistant, Linda Currier, was the unofficial social director at TALX. She would bring in the birthday cake once a month, set things up to celebrate the Cardinals' home openers, and arrange everything for our Popcorn Thursdays.

But her biggest social event every year was the Christmas party. I gave her a modest budget and asked her to do what she could to make the event special. She would go all out, never ceasing to amaze everyone. There was a big warehouse toward the back of one of our offices where one year Linda spent hours after the office closed, painting snowmen, Christmas trees, and snowflakes on the walls. The day of the party, she cut out black boot-prints and made a path that led down to the warehouse where we held the party. We had a big spread of food. I loved leading everyone in singing Christmas carols—dressed in appropriate holiday costumes. I always enjoyed the reaction I got from the room when they saw the costumes I was wearing. Sometimes it was my Santa outfit or, my personal favorite, the elf costume, with bright red-and-green tights and a red tunic and hat, complete with jingle bells. I used a photo of me as an elf as my Gmail account photo for quite a few years after I retired. I think I cherished that costume and photo because deep down that was the persona I wanted people to remember when they thought about my time with the company.

Jim, Tom, and Sally weren't quite as fond of the elf costume as I was. However, I'm not one to shy away from good-natured criticism and even light ribbing. Getting in front of a room of hundreds of people, looking a little foolish, is an excellent way to let people know you don't take life so seriously. When I wore a costume in front of a room full of TALX employees, I hoped it helped me shed the CEO persona that created an imagined barrier. I hoped it gave them permission not to let life become too serious. At TALX, we nurtured a family-friendly and fun environment because I wanted to take care of the people who were handpicked and brought up in the company. I was told I could be a bit intimidating, and as the company grew and younger folks came in, I learned they were a little afraid of me. That's a natural reaction, but when I broke out in song in a meeting or came bouncing into a company party with an elf costume decked with jingling, silver bells, it always evoked a smile. I knew I'd cultivated a positive, fun atmosphere when they'd fondly acknowledge, "It's just Bill, again."

Humor, in tasteful forms, was an essential ingredient in the TALX culture. We made sure we had fun! But singing and playing music kept our spirits lifted through the challenging times.

Chapter 8
X'S AND O'S

Just as a successful football coach uses X's and O's on a chalk board to communicate the game plan to the team, planning for the success of a new venture or a new project is the most important step a person can take to prepare a business for growth and prosperity. If we as executors of this new endeavor don't plan, our vendors, our customers, and our employees will plan for us. They will dictate our policies, our projects, what we sell, what to pay us, and when they will pay us. I've seen this happen without fail. Without a good plan, chaos will occur.

Over the years of starting new businesses, I've discovered that planning must be straightforward and practical. It must give the executives and management a clear, strategic path to channel the energy of the entire organization.

I've used different iterations of my planning model. I first developed it out of necessity in the school of hard knocks. Then, before I was forty, I joined Young Presidents' Organization (YPO), where I learned how to construct a workable plan that could drive an entire organization.

The method starts by pulling a select group of key people, usually less than ten, into a room and setting the tone: "You're in here for at least a day. Maybe a day and a half or two days. And we're going to work together to figure out who we are and where we're going."

The sessions are an intense examination of the organization's current situation and future prospects. We begin by asking a series of questions. Here are some of them:

- What are we doing today? What are the results we are getting?
- What do we know about our customers' needs/problems?
- What do we want to be? What do we want to do in the future?
- Why are we in business?

To stimulate conversation, we record the different thoughts on flip charts, using phrases or single words that capture the essence of the answers that come from the group.

During the discussion, I listen, clarify, and allow the ideas to flow. We then begin to build a series of statements. These statements begin to shape a plan that will result in a direction for the company that builds on the strength of the organization and the demands and opportunities of the marketplace. Articulating and documenting what you want to be and what products and services you want to develop and sell inevitably focuses everyone on what the organization should be concentrating on. It also allows the management team to quickly say no to opportunities that may come along that don't fit the plan or that will be a distraction to the agreed-upon direction. In short, a good strategic plan allows the organization to "keep the main thing the main thing."

While the structure of a strategic plan looks fundamental, if it's well-thought-out, the simplicity allows for a consistent message throughout the organization. Here is the structure I like for a strategic plan:

The Elements of a Strategic Plan

Vision statement: A brief statement (approximately fifteen to twenty-five words) communicating what the organization **intends to be**. The vision statement is intended to have a time horizon of five to ten years.

Examples: To be the leader in quality and value in the heavy construction equipment industry, or

To be as good looking as Tom Cruise.

Mission statement: A brief statement (approximately ten to twenty words) communicating what the organization **plans**

to do. Mission statements are designed to have a time horizon of three to six years. If the mission gets wordy, make it concise and create sub-thoughts in a different document.

Examples: To build a regional, then national, sales and service organization that creates consistent 15 percent growth in revenue, year over year, or

To exercise and lose weight to create a new image.

Goals: Prioritized statements of desired accomplishments that can be completed in the next twelve months (usually no more than six or seven main goals). Goals should have the following qualities:

- They are **consistent** with the **vision** and **mission**.
- They contain a **completion date**.
- They include a quantitative value that is **measurable**.
- They are written down and visible (e.g., posted on walls).
- They have the consensus of the organization.
- They have an assigned responsibility (a person or a team).
- They have a defined feedback process.

Examples: By March 1, hire three new experienced salespeople to sell geographically to construction companies within four hundred miles of our headquarters. Responsibility = VP of Sales, or

By year's end, lose twenty pounds and run a six-minute mile, as measured on the scale and by a stopwatch.

Strategies: These are key actions that will be taken to accomplish each goal.

Examples: Interview three recruiting companies and pick one to help execute our hiring activity, or

Join a workout facility and start on a healthy diet program.

Feedback: Develop a frequent and regular review (no less than monthly) of the progress toward achieving each goal. If there are shortfalls, reexamine the strategies for their effectiveness. The feedback mechanism is usually part of a metric reporting process.

Example: I like to use a "stoplight" approach to this feedback report, using colored circles to indicate the current status. A circle filled with green means "on schedule," yellow means "needs attention," and red means "seriously behind schedule." With this system, management can quickly determine where to focus their attention: change the team, change the strategies, or change the goal?

Without a regular system of feedback, it's difficult to maintain momentum toward accomplishing the goals.

Christian Principles as a Management Strategy

I didn't initially formulate my planning strategy as the result of my faith. But by the time I became involved with Interface

Technology, I'd become more knowledgeable about the Bible and what it teaches. I discovered that **God is a planner**.

When we plan our steps, it allows God to step in and direct us in providential ways we could never imagine. It makes me think of that proverb, "The mind of man plans his way, but the LORD directs his steps" (Prov. 16:9 NASB). God expects us to plan our way and not to go into an endeavor haphazardly. With a plan in our hearts, it's easier to recognize the providential hand of our Creator at work directing us in new ways.

The Payoff

As much as I knew the importance of planning and the value of having a clear direction for our operations, I never imagined the payoff that would come down the road from utilizing this planning model.

In 1988, I became CEO of a floundering Interface Technology. Over the course of the first few years, I listened and learned from the people who were driving the sales and product-development efforts. The company was in trouble. Despite a promising technology involving voice, data, and computers, it wasn't profitable to the point that investors would stay engaged much longer. At some point in the 1990–1991 timeframe, I implemented this strategic planning process with the key staff in an attempt to retool the company's customer and product focus. We needed a workable plan that we thought would produce better results than we were getting.

We conducted a series of planning sessions with key individuals, using the above method, and asked ourselves a series of questions. Among them were these:

- What do we want to be?
- What are we doing well today?
- Where do we think the market is going for what our skills are?
- Is there a niche that we can build upon?
- What is the competitive environment in that niche?

It became very clear what the company had to do to survive. We renamed the company TALX, because we allowed people to "talk" to computers via the touch-tone telephone. We decided to focus our sales efforts on the human resource departments of our clients and prospects, because we had solutions that were selling well. We needed to turn some of the customized solutions we had already sold to this market into service applications that would produce a source of reliable, recurring revenue. While we had a few ideas on how to accomplish this, I wanted the senior staff to have ownership, so I had them communicate our mission and vision to every employee, particularly the sales staff. By so doing, a creative impulse was unleashed that went far beyond what we, as a small planning team, could accomplish on our own.

Chapter 9
PROVIDENCE

The story of how I got involved with TALX includes a Providential event, an incident that I believe was directed by God. After Citicorp bought FDS, I started a venture capital and management firm called Intech Group. My goal was to find existing companies, or new ideas that could become companies, in St. Louis. In that venture, I invested in a couple of small firms and provided management support for the CEOs. Through Intech, I started a new business called Noetic Technologies. I went to the Washington University School of Engineering and met with Jim McKelvey, head of the engineering school. He told me about some research in the civil engineering department that had promise. McDonnell Douglas was the sponsoring company. After looking into it, I concluded this technology transfer from academia to the business world would be an interesting venture.

Soon, we formed Noetic Technologies to advance and sell a finite element design software, called the "H Version." I raised additional capital from a venture firm in St. Louis, hired several sales, management, and technical people, and Noetic was off and running. Although it was a "sell or die" business model, the company was successful, and four years later, MacNeal-Schwendler, a CAD/CAM engineering company listed on the NASDAQ, purchased Noetic. We had granted shares to Washington University, as well as to the professor who had guided the development. All the shareholders in Noetic benefited from the sale.

After a few years of buying and selling companies and doing consulting, I got restless. I had a desire to manage something again, and I found myself uneasy and frustrated in a transactional role. Here is where God stepped in.

In the late spring of 1987, Sally and I were preparing for a Florida vacation when, out of the blue, I received a call from Paul Cornelson, the CEO of MiTek Industries. Paul and his board had been struggling to make their investment in a small software company, Interface Technology (later to be known as TALX), profitable. Someone, I don't know who, told him he needed to talk to me. Interface was losing money, "bleeding cash," with no growth. He asked me to observe the company, get to know the people and the business, and then provide his team with insights and recommendations. While Sally and I were in Florida, I thought it over. I thought this opportunity with MiTek might provide a new beginning for me. On our return, I agreed to go to Interface for a couple of weeks and give Paul some observations. While there, I recognized some solid competencies in Interface's technology, including the use of the touch-tone telephone to deliver and receive data with a computer. This technology was called audio response.

I had become familiar with audio response from my days at IBM. Interface put information at the caller's fingertips via the touch-tone telephone. One of the early uses was in the banking industry. Customers could call a special telephone number, enter their account number and listen to their balances and recent transactions. Interface was selling its own design of audio response hardware and developing software solutions to solve problems for an impressive list of customers. The application solutions were based on the customer's unique needs.

For example, they built a system for a major airline to provide flight arrival and departure information. They created a different system to record customer orders for pay-per-view movies and sporting events for a cable TV company, and an on-demand sales and inventory status tracking and inquiry system for a major beer company. And that was just to name a few of the large, unique solutions they developed. All of these were individual, customized systems that were not applicable to the next customer, even one in the same industry.

Once a solution was installed and paid for, they needed to sell and develop the next one. It was the same "sell or die" business model we had at FDS in the beginning. If they sold a solution and got it installed, the bills were paid for a few months. But if sales slowed, so did cash flow, and that created stressful situations.

I felt changes might be necessary to make the company sustainable and give it the chance to grow. But what changes? Arguably, the annual maintenance contracts sold to each customer as part of the original sale were good revenue, but they offered a minimal profit margin and were not enough to sustain the company during a slow sales cycle.

I made my report to Paul and his board. I was so "enamored of" and fascinated with the problem needing to be solved that I proposed an agreement with MiTek that would provide me with an option to purchase a portion of the company. That option would give me the opportunity to invest money, if the business turned around. MiTek would continue to keep the company solvent. With some negotiation, MiTek agreed. Little did I know that this company, almost twenty years later, was to become the gold star of my entrepreneurial efforts.

It took a few months for me to wind up some activities with Intech, and early in 1988 I took over as president. During my early time at Interface, I focused on understanding the people and the business, learning more about their unique technology, talking to customers, and eliminating some expenses.

From my FDS days, I had learned a business principle that shaped the rest of my career:

Building recurring revenue into your business model is critical for long-term survival and growth.

As had been the case at FDS, I realized Interface needed to develop a reliable stream of recurring revenue to make the company stable and give it the chance to grow, something more than the software maintenance contracts.

One of the first things I did when I took the reins at Interface was to hire some new sales staff, including a man named Tom Kellett. I worked with the entire sales force to shift the way we approached solving our customers' problems. We lost a few sales folks in the process of change, as they didn't feel they could be successful in the new model. We slowly began moving from the customized "sell or die" model to one where we developed solutions with broader appeal, offering them as a service, paid for by a monthly fee. The service applications were run on our in-house computers instead of being housed on the customer's premises. We managed the system; the customers just used it.

We constantly talked about uncovering problems that weren't unique to the individual client and how that could become a service with multiple customers. It was a lot less expensive to solve the same problem for several customers, both for us and the customer. We could charge a low price for the service to multiple customers on a long-term contract basis (three-year minimum). Also, we could reduce our development effort, and the customer didn't have to invest in software and hardware.

Turning a Corner

By late 1990, we had made the first shift into a fledgling recurring revenue system. We converted one of our custom benefits-enrollment and provider-verification software solutions into a stable revenue source. We removed any customer-specific provisions and created a "feature table" to handle customer differences. Features could be turned on or off based on customer needs. We operated the service on our computers and charged an affordable fee for each transaction.

I believed we were on an upward trajectory regarding revenue growth, so I exercised my option to purchase and became a major shareholder in Interface. But we still hadn't turned the corner to long-term profitability.

In 1991, with the help of Hughes Advertising, we changed our name to TALX, suggesting that we made computers "TALK." Jack Hughes, my friend and president of Hughes Advertising, led this effort.

After the name change, we began to focus on selling additional applications to the human resource departments of corporate America. When possible, we sold the service, rather than software and hardware.

I was sitting at my desk in early 1994 when Tom Kellett walked into my office with an idea. We didn't know it that day, but his idea would take what had been a floundering company and eventually make it worth hundreds of millions.

Tom was part of what had become an outstanding sales team. He was constantly on the hunt for new ways to solve customers' problems. On the day he came into my office, he had just returned from calling on customers on the West Coast, where he learned about a problem facing one of our clients, McDonnell Douglas. They were experiencing a drain on their human resources department from employment verification phone calls. We soon learned that Coca-Cola and Texaco had the same problem.

It was a standard procedure in human resource departments that employment verification was a manual process, handled by phone, and it interrupted the normal flow of daily work. The demand for verifications by financial firms was increasing quickly. A growing number of retailers and restaurants were starting to accept major credit cards because of the growth of an online, national credit processing system. This meant more Americans were applying for credit cards than before, and those credit card companies required employment and income verification as part of their review process. The same was true for home loans. Add to that, the human resources departments across the country, which could not keep up with the demand for prior employment information as their former employees applied for new jobs. A company's current and prior employees who needed credit or jobs were getting poor service because of the HR department's inability to respond to the flood of calls in a timely manner.

During Tom's typical fact-finding interview to discuss the key issues they were facing, McDonnell Douglas staff related how they had a small team trying to figure out a solution to keep up with the exploding demand, but they hadn't been successful yet. The best option they could come up with was for the human resources department to dedicate a four-hour-per-week window to answer verification calls. While it controlled the time their team spent on the phones, it wasn't an adequate solution, because many callers got a busy signal. McDonnell Douglas was worried that the volume of calls would increase after their next major round of layoffs, compounding the problem.

Tom listened to McDonnell Douglas and then heard the same scenario from other TALX sales people calling on Texaco and Coca-Cola. To his credit, he immediately recognized the need for an automated solution, sold as a service, to all three companies.

TALX could invest in development resources once, but, like the other human resource solutions we'd been building for service, we could sell the solution several times. As we began to plan, the potential for Tom's idea slowly began to take shape and the possibilities began to grow. I sensed he had touched on an issue affecting more than just the three companies he knew about. It was a brilliant idea. I became excited about the prospects this held for our clients and our company. I had a growing sense this could be the recurring revenue solution we'd been searching for.

I knew we were potentially onto something big, something innovative, that had *not* been done before. I didn't want to chance missing any key pieces of the problem, so I joined Tom at his next meeting with McDonnell Douglas, and I was able to get a broader view of their challenges. After we met several more times, we jointly decided that the St. Louis division of McDonnell Douglas would be a natural fit to help us build, test, and deploy the solution.

We certainly understood what the customer needed. I also had a vision that we needed to develop a service that could be used by any company to verify employment and income for their employees. All indicators were that demand for verifications for credit cards, car loans, and mortgages would continue to grow. So the need for verification services would continue to expand. But the question became, How did we structure an approach that all corporations would willingly use by furnishing us data on their employees? Realizing that we were the first to automate this application—pioneers, so to speak—we anticipated some sales resistance to joining. We decided to offer the service for free for a period of time as a pilot. We decided that the service wasn't going to cost the employer one cent, as long as they agreed to submit their employees' records on a payroll cycle basis. We would then have the data on a database, continuously updated with each payroll cycle.

We overcame the privacy issues with employers by providing an automated system for employees to receive a security code. For a lender or credit company to receive verification on an employee, they needed a verification code. Companies were then willing to submit data records to the system on all employees because their employees could authorize the use of their own data when they needed a verification. The system lifted the burden of verification calls from the human resource department. Employers were required to stop providing verifications to callers. Instead, they needed to put a prerecorded message on the telephone, referring the caller to an automated telephone service for the information they needed.

We designed a three-part system:

1. The credit-granting agencies, the verifiers who needed the data, would pay for the verification on a fee-per-call basis, using a 1-900 number.
2. TALX provided and maintained the database and voice-response system on our secure computers.

3. The employers, who were charged nothing, provided the data, updated after each payroll period to maintain currency.

Bingo! It was a win-win scenario for everyone, and the fees from the AT&T 1-900 verification line became the recurring revenue model we had been looking for.

We called the service "The Work Number for Everyone." We later added internet access, on a subscription basis, which bypassed the phone, and sent out monthly invoices. We kept the 1-900 capability. We dropped the "for Everyone" from the service name, shortening the service name to "The Work Number." While we understood the potential immediately, our success would ride on how quickly we could create the system and grow the database of employment records. Initially I used contract programmers because our in-house programmers were committed to completing the custom programs that were still the primary revenue source for the company. Gradually, the contract staff became smaller and our in-house programming staff working on The Work Number development became larger.

We added new sales people to sell The Work Number, giving them geographic territories covering the entire United States. We retained some of the existing sales personnel to sell other human resource services and customer-premise systems. When we launched the 1-900 number in 1995, we had about thirty-five thousand records on our database from our test clients. We usually closed sales with employers, generally in one or two sales calls. We were offering a free service that would transfer the cost of verifications from the employers, who were hard-pressed to complete them for the verifiers, who needed the data. The service would also improve the turnaround time for employees to get the financial transaction they had applied for. Before long the database grew to over 10 million employee records. We decided to always offer the service to employers for free, as long as they were sending us regular payroll data updates.

Chapter 10
INTO THE PUBLIC ARENA

By mid-1996, we knew The Work Number was the future of the company. We were adding new companies regularly and generating an encouraging amount of revenue. Yet it was still a fledgling project.

Our new corporate emphasis on The Work Number marked a huge shift for the company—not only in the way we sold and supported our products, but also in our company culture and workforce.

We were facing a significant paradigm shift, disrupting the course of our business. We were in a situation where we were anticipating a dip in our cash flow because sales of customer-premise systems, where we sold hardware and software to run at the customers' offices, were slowing as we gradually moved staff to the "Software as a Service" business model. In this model, customers got the same capability they desired without making a capital outlay, and TALX received monthly recurring revenue by delivering the service. It turns out we were at the forefront of the movement. The new service business direction, however, created a problem for small companies like TALX. We needed cash to support the company during the period while software revenue declined and fledgling service business revenue grew. After exploring several options for raising money, including venture capital, loans, and the investors in TALX, we had a board meeting in mid-1996 to discuss our alternatives. Confident in the recurring revenue stream and the success The Work Number promised, we decided to pursue an initial public offering (IPO) to take TALX public. Having handled all financial needs privately in the past, this was a *big* step! Some parts of the company didn't fit our new focus. Langenbacher Document Services and EKI Yellow Pages businesses were sold. These were companies I had owned from Intech Group days, learned from, and brought with me when I'd joined TALX. Although these businesses were profitable, they represented a drain on our staff and management time, and a diversion from our newly defined business.

The TALX board included Dick Ford, Gene Toombs, Steve Yoakum, Tony Holcombe, and me, as chairman. They were all excellent businessmen, but adding another board member, one with experience running a public company, made sense. We invited Craig LaBarge, president of LaBarge Industries, to join our board. We began to interview several investment bankers, who gave us the confidence to go for it, and hired two firms. They proceeded to "dress us up" and update our investor presentation. They helped us organize our financials in a way that would emphasize the value of the growing service revenue. Then Craig Cohen, our CFO at the time, and I were off for a road show to tell our story. The investment bankers made the appointments. We called on investment brokers, mutual funds, family investment groups, and any other organization that our bankers thought would be interested in investing in our story. We visited potential investors in most major cities in the US, plus London and Zurich. We were gone for three or four weeks, with short visits home to repack our suitcases.

The structure of the appointments was scripted; we had one hour to show our slides, tell the story of TALX, and the future potential of The Work Number. We would talk for about twenty to twenty-five minutes, which left the balance of the hour for questions from the participants. We barely had time to reflect on our performance and the investors' reactions before it was time for the next meeting. It was exhausting! But it was exhilarating.

On October 15, 1996, we were back in St. Louis, and I sat down with the TALX board on a conference call with the investment bankers who had run the road show. They had talked to the potential investors regarding their interest. They analyzed the feedback and gave us an estimate that we could sell a million shares in the company at nine dollars per share when the markets opened the next morning. We had hoped for eleven or twelve. After a little bit of discussion, we gave the go-ahead, and on the morning of October 16, NASDAQ approved our stock symbol, "TALX," and trading began. That morning, I pulled the whole TALX family into a meeting room to tell them the good news, and later we celebrated with the bankers who had gotten us through the overwhelming and taxing process. But our work was far from over, and the pressure didn't lift.

The next morning, I woke up to a different business reality. Now that TALX was public, we had a large group of investors to answer to, and we had quarterly forecasts we had presented on the road. Public scrutiny requires a different type of performance standard, and it was one that would take some getting used to. I thought we could manage it, but it was definitely going to take a shift in thinking. While we had been on the road show, I had lost touch with what was really going on at TALX. When I came back to the office, I gave myself time to catch up, and I quickly became aware that I needed to focus on how we should operate moving forward. Our customer-premise sales were dismal. I needed to rethink our business to make it respond to the changes that were occurring, namely a faster-than-anticipated decline in our software sales and encouraging incremental growth of The Work Number. The Work Number database was growing faster than the transaction volume. It turned out that the verifiers, the potential users of the service, needed more education, and some of our employers were still responding to verification request calls, even though they were not supposed to. I concluded that TALX would require some major organizational changes and downsizing.

Our sales organization was divided between those who had experienced success in selling customer-premise systems and those focused on selling The Work Number and our other human resource services. Our customer service and product development organizations were divided in two groups as well.

I realized we needed to reduce the numbers and align the majority of our staff to The Work Number. I spent a few days sorting my thoughts on three-by-five cards and then had a meeting with key people throughout the organization. For two days, I had people from sales, customer service, human resources, finance, and The Work Number team meet off-site to discuss how we could get our organization in line with where it needed to be. We used flip charts and developed new job titles, decided which people stayed and which needed to move on, and how those who stayed could be most effective. We dramatically reduced the sales force that sold customer-premise systems and slightly increased the sales staff who would sell services and The Work Number. We did the same determination with our customer service and development staffs. Our organization was now structured for the recurring revenue of services to HR departments including The Work Number.

I might have made it sound easy, but it was gut-wrenching! I was creating havoc in the lives of those talented employees who would no longer be with us. I was a bear at home, and I had to be an encouraging cheerleader at the office.

By the end of the first quarter, after we went public (the end of 1996), we had reduced ongoing expenses considerably. We had noticeably flattened the development and support organization, bringing me in direct contact with each element of the business. Our former sales manager had resigned, and I became the interim sales manager. This turned out to be very beneficial, as I could personally mold our sales team in the new direction and observe customer reactions. We were selling smaller dollar-value services like The Work Number to more clients. Our developers now focused on creating systems that could handle high-volume transactional activity. We changed the role of our customer service group so that they could develop long-lasting relationships with our service customers, instead of a short relationship that lasted only as long as the installation period for the customer-premises systems. During this exercise, we reduced the staff and ongoing expenses by about 30 percent.

Before all of the organizational changes and reduced expenses could have an impact on our financials, we had to file our first quarter report. We reported a sizable loss. I learned the hard way that one does *not* plan on going public, and *then* rearrange its business model, resulting in a substantial loss, just *after* going public. You reorganize beforehand! Our new investors were not prepared for a shortfall in our growth. The market is never patient with companies that don't meet their projections. In February of 1997, I watched with horror as our stock price plummeted from its initial price of nine dollars a share, wavering at or below three dollars a share.

My world at work and at home flipped upside down. It was an awful time; we had friends who had invested in the company and had taken losses, and both Sally and I had to face those people. I was answering calls from investment analysts asking me why in the world this had happened, and what did I plan to do about it. It was a painful time for TALX, and for Sally and me, but I was steadfast in my belief in the strength of The Work Number. Fortunately, I had already taken action, so I could communicate some ray of hope. I knew that getting wrapped up in what had already occurred—"woulda, shoulda, coulda"—was not productive, and that focusing on the promise and strategy of The Work Number was what would help us recover. That is what I believed and what I told everyone throughout it all.

The last half of 1997 and the first half of 1998 brought much success to The Work Number. We were signing up employers at a good pace. The transactions, which generated our revenue, increased nicely as well. I felt I needed to address the financial community face to face and explain the cause of our failure and the subsequent actions we were taking and remind them of the encouraging recent results. I needed to rekindle their interest in TALX. I invited many of the analysts that covered us to come to St. Louis for a meeting. Quite a few responded that they would come.

The meeting was at a downtown ballroom in the summer of 1998. I knew it was going to be difficult looking into the faces of the crowd. I had to admit that mistakes had been made, and that some of the people in the room had been let down. I began the meeting by reading the following poem:

If— by Rudyard Kipling

If you can keep your head when all about you
    Are losing theirs and blaming it on you,
If you can trust yourself when all men doubt you,
    But make allowance for their doubting too;
If you can wait and not be tired by waiting,
    Or being lied about, don't deal in lies,
Or being hated, don't give way to hating,
    And yet don't look too good, nor talk too wise:

If you can dream—and not make dreams your master;
    If you can think—and not make thoughts your aim;
If you can meet with Triumph and Disaster
    And treat those two impostors just the same;
If you can bear to hear the truth you've spoken
Twisted by knaves to make a trap for fools,
Or watch the things you gave your life to, broken,
    And stoop and build 'em up with worn-out tools:

INTO THE PUBLIC ARENA

If you can make one heap of all your winnings
    And risk it on one turn of pitch-and-toss,
And lose, and start again at your beginnings
    And never breathe a word about your loss;
If you can force your heart and nerve and sinew
    To serve your turn long after they are gone,
And so hold on when there is nothing in you
    Except the Will which says to them: 'Hold on!'

If you can talk with crowds and keep your virtue,
    Or walk with Kings—nor lose the common, touch
If neither foes nor loving friends can hurt you,
    If all men count with you, but none too much;
If you can fill the unforgiving minute
    With sixty seconds' worth of distance run,
Yours is the Earth and everything that's in it,
    And—which is more—you'll be a Man, my son!

As I finished reading Kipling's poem, I allowed the silence that filled the room to hang for a moment. I looked out onto a sea of investment bankers and securities analysts who had flown to St. Louis to ask questions and learn more about our financial future. Reading the poem took some of the tension out of the room, and out of me. I explained our failures, which, I told them, were really my failures. After the meeting, several people commended me for facing up to the situation we were in. They were encouraged by what I said about the future.

In early 1999, TALX was growing nicely. The database of employment records was steadily increasing as sales successes occurred. Inquiries, which generated our revenue for The Work Number, increased faster than the database, as new verifying industries discovered the value of The Work Number. We added a new sales force to sell to these verifying markets, the people who needed the data.

Later in 1999, as our growth continued to accelerate, I started searching for new ways to add data to our database, in addition to our in-house sales channel. I discovered the unemployment claims processing market segment. Nationally, fifteen to twenty different companies processed unemployment claims with the goal of reducing an employer's financial liability. These companies would approve the legitimate claims and fight the fraudulent ones. To do this, they needed data records on their customers' employees. These data records were similar to those The Work Number required to process verifications. I visited most of the claims processing companies in the country, twelve or thirteen of them, and worked out a partnership agreement with a few of them. Since we used the same information, it just seemed logical that we could work together for our mutual benefit. The unemployment companies would offer The Work Number service to their customers, and TALX would compensate them for the successful referral.

Our growth was such that in early 2001, we decided to do a secondary offering to raise additional funds. This is similar to an IPO process, but the company is already public. There is no bargaining with the investors, as the price of the shares is determined by the marketplace. We completed the secondary offering in August of 2001. Our timing was unfortunate. The attack on the World Trade Center buildings on September 11, 2001, slowed business and new customer decisions to a crawl. Several large client contracts were delayed. Our financial report for the quarter ending September 30, 2001, was disappointing. We decided to lump all of the bad news into this one quarterly report. We took a one-time charge to write off the remains of our customer-premises software business. The combination of the slowed business and write-off was not appreciated by the investment community. We obviously hadn't heeded the lesson of timing from our IPO. We had dug ourselves another hole we needed to claw our way out of!

Before the end of 2001, the Securities and Exchange Commission (SEC) began an investigation, and a stockholder class action lawsuit was filed. We did not feel the SEC had a good case against us. We had not deceived anyone. Our actions were logical, but possibly naïve, under the circumstances.

The SEC investigation lingered for several years. In late 2003, they levied fines against me and our CFO, Craig Cohen. Craig resigned and fought the SEC until he won; his case was dismissed. I felt I didn't have the time or energy to fight, so I paid a negotiated fine without admitting to any irregularities. Through it all, I told our attorneys to keep me informed of how the cases were progressing, but that I intended to focus my energies on running and growing the company.

The lawyers handled the legal issues, and we had business insurance to insulate us from financial damages, so we went back to what we did best—servicing our customers and building the business. As our organization refocused and grew, our success began to show. The employment verification transaction market was growing, and competition was popping up—a sure sign we were headed in the right direction. The Work Number was outperforming even our best-case estimates. Our recent quarterly reports were showing nice progress.

Chapter 11
A STROKE OF GENIUS!

Meanwhile, I realized that our partnerships with companies in the unemployment claims processing market weren't providing the business lift for The Work Number that I had anticipated. For those partners, getting contracts for The Work Number from their customers was not as high a priority as it was for TALX. So, I became a one-man mergers and acquisition department.

The industry was profitable and had long-term contracts with its clients (recurring revenue). The companies were privately held and generally had only a few stockholders. Acquiring several of those companies would change their priority toward The Work Number, because we would have management control. Additionally, we would be acquiring stable additions, with profitable recurring revenue, to our business. Late in 2001, I approached the two largest companies, the Frick Company in St. Louis, Missouri, and a division of Gates McDonald Insurance in Columbus, Ohio. These companies collectively represented about 35 percent of the industry volume. They were arch enemies, due to the decades-long competitive nature of the industry. It was clear they disliked each other. Separately, they both expressed a willingness to discuss acquisition. The Frick team in my meetings consisted of four or five members of their senior management who all owned a significant portion of their employee stock ownership plan, or ESOP. They all participated in the discussions. The Gates team was two men from the parent insurance firm and two senior managers of the unemployment division. None of this team had any ownership interests. Therefore, their negotiations were mostly logistical, whereas the Frick team was very price oriented.

As I negotiated with each team, I had an interesting idea. I met with my new CFO, Keith Graves, and told him I wanted to buy these two companies *on the same day*.

"Why?" he asked, rather skeptically.

I told him I thought that because of the enmity between these two companies and the competitive nature within the industry, if we bought one, we'd never get the other. I wanted them both. So we needed to buy them on the same day, in such a way that neither knew about the acquisition of the other until the deals were complete. Keith and I had meetings with our attorneys and investment bankers (we needed to borrow money for the purchases) to test the feasibility of the idea. Most thought it was a little crazy, but they said we were the client, and they would try to please us.

After some extended negotiations with each of the firms, we agreed on a purchase price to buy each one. We created a pro forma of the combined businesses showing what we expected TALX to look like financially after the acquisitions were complete. The pro forma was convincing, and we got the loans we needed. I set two closing dates; one was at 9 a.m. in the offices of our attorneys, Bryan Cave, on the twenty-first floor, and the other was at 10 a.m. in their offices in the same building, but on the fifteenth floor.

On the day of closing, in March of 2002, we had two teams of lawyers from our firm, one in each of the closing rooms. Keith and I were there to greet the 9 a.m. group and their attorneys, and at 10 a.m. to greet the other group and their lawyers. We started the closing process, and we wandered back and forth between the closing rooms, answering questions and negotiating last-minute requests. I had told each company that when their closing was complete, we would meet at the TALX offices for lunch and have discussions about the future.

When the first group arrived at our offices, all was well. When the second company arrived, the room got quiet and cold. Lunch was cordial, but not interactive between the two groups. The meeting following lunch was interesting. I had prepared a series of thoughts on how these companies might work together. There were about ten or twelve different areas of the business we needed to have managed by one or the other company, reducing redundancy. We were going to form study teams to help choose the best practices between the two in each business area. We set dates for follow-up and scheduled another meeting in a week.

To my surprise, during that next week, the two senior members of the management team from Gates resigned and refused to participate—evidence of the animosity I had detected. They thought the best practices decisions were already slanted toward Frick, due to their St. Louis location. So their resignation brought about what they feared; the best practice areas all defaulted to Frick. Two of the larger areas of redundancy were the management teams and the computers used to run the services. The resignations of the Gates pair had solved the management redundancy issue. Gates McDonald, the insurance company, who owned the computers in Columbus, was happy with the freed-up time on its computers by having the unemployment claims processing switched to the Frick computers in St. Louis. Thus, the computer redundancy situation was also solved. I still believe we would not have acquired both unemployment entities without the bold decision to secretly orchestrate the closing of both deals on the same day.

The security analysts who covered TALX loved the result. It was innovative! The analysts needed some education, however, because this industry had been private and under the public market radar. TALX annual revenues more than doubled in one day. Our profitability jumped as well, and our database very soon added millions of new records, with the potential for millions more. Because we bought these companies at multiples less than the market valuation of TALX at the time, our stock price appreciated. We subsequently made several other smaller unemployment business acquisitions, using a similar formula of buying at lesser multiples than the market was giving us. Each acquisition saw an increase in our stock price. Keith Graves was very involved in all of this, and he and his team were extremely valuable in smoothly integrating each of the acquisitions. The original partnerships we had with several of the unemployment claims processing companies we did not acquire were dissolved.

The next several years were busy consolidating the unemployment businesses and growing The Work Number database. We had come through a major crisis and had not only survived but had learned and grown stronger. My friend and Bryan Cave attorney, Walter Metcalfe, said I have "no rearview mirror," because I do not dwell on the past but learn and move forward. The SEC issues had been complicated and emotionally draining, but I could not let them disrupt the excitement and magnitude of the work ahead.

Chapter 12
A "SAAS-Y" CONNECTION

In the fall of 2002, I received a phone call from Steve Singh, the president of Concur Technologies. Concur, located in Seattle, Washington, was a successful and profitable firm, providing "Travel Expense Management" software to corporations nationwide. Employees could use a touch-tone phone or the internet to enter their travel expenses. Not only would this system capture the expense data easier and quicker, it would provide analysis reporting of travel expenses to help the corporations negotiate discounts.

Concur had been public for more than ten years. Steve had the idea that he wanted more service revenue, rather than continuing to rely on software sales. He called on some of the same security analysts in New York and Boston that I had, updating them on the company status. The analysts were one of the main drivers in a stock's buying and selling activity. As Steve, on a trip to visit analysts, discussed his thoughts, one of them remembered that TALX had successfully managed a similar business change. TALX had made the organizational changes necessary to convert to a "Software as a Service" (recurring revenue) company, and Steve wanted to pick my brain about the changes we made—those that worked and those that didn't.

We set up a time for Steve to come to St. Louis for a visit. We spent an entire morning talking, and at the end of our meeting Steve asked me to join his board of directors. He wanted my experience and he had a board seat available. The next day I called him and accepted the board position, effective in early 2003, and made an immediate purchase of Concur stock. My investment value grew because the stock increased in value, and I received stock options as compensation for being on the board.

Steve and I were running companies with similar business models, using our software to provide service to our customers. We were part of a fledgling trend among technology companies to change to that model. After a few years, our business model, which we called "Software as a Service," became legitimate when the market gave it a new name: "SaaS," pronounced "sass," as in *sassy*.

I served on Concur's board for seven years, retiring in 2010. It was a great experience. I met some smart people and learned much. In 2014, Concur was acquired by SAP.

Chapter 13
HITTING A HOME RUN!

I suspect that the dream of many young men and women is to own their own business that provides independence and financial security. The free enterprise system we have in America certainly allows that to happen. But it takes hard work, courage, perseverance in the face of failure, and a lot of God's blessing before a dream can come to fruition. One must be able to make the tough decisions of changing direction and cutting staff when the expenses are greater than the revenue. It is hard to see a future opportunity when the present is dismal.

But ten years after we launched The Work Number, despite our financial fumbles, federal government regulatory issues, and stockholder unrest, TALX had amassed a sizable database. We had focused for years on building that database, knowing that our revenue would grow as the number of data records grew. The database was a helpful tool for human resource managers, pre-employment screeners, mortgage lenders, credit card issuers, and government clients, to name a few. In that database, we had millions of people, where they worked and for how long, how much money they made, and their job titles.

Eventually, we caught the eye of Equifax, one of the big three credit-reporting agencies. Their vice president of United States Credit Information Services (USCIS), Dann Adams, scheduled a meeting to investigate using our data in their credit-reporting business. Equifax was trying to find ways to get an edge over their competition and knowing that every loan application needed to verify the employment records that The Work Number housed, they wanted to be able to provide data that their competitors, Trans Union and Experian, could not. Having access to an applicant's employment information would allow Equifax to provide credit reports to their customers, primarily lenders, that would give more detailed insights into an individual borrower's risk than Trans Union and Experian could provide.

Dann came to St. Louis to learn and to discuss how we could work together. He met with several of our sales and operations staff. He left saying he was impressed with what he'd learned, and the next time he came out, he brought Rick Smith, the new CEO of Equifax, with him. This was a sales opportunity for us, so I wasn't in the meeting, but we all knew this was a potentially big deal, so I was aware of what was going on and asked everyone to keep me up to speed. I also asked the team to let me know when the meeting with Dann and Rick was closing so I could meet them in the front lobby and give a quick hello. When I met them, I thanked them for coming out and told them I hoped they were pleased with what they learned. In chatting informally with Rick, I discovered that we were both Purdue graduates and members of the same chapter of the Sigma Chi fraternity. I graduated twenty years before Rick. We had a nice talk about our alma mater and an upcoming fundraising project to rebuild our fraternity's house. We discovered that both of our pictures were in the fundraising brochure. Then Rick and Dann headed back to Atlanta.

To my surprise, I got a call several weeks later from Rick Smith. He said he was coming back to see us and would like to talk to me about a partnership with Equifax. He went on to tell me how impressed he was with our culture and the people he'd met, and from a data standpoint, it was a fit for their business. He said that after meeting with us, he and Dann were confident that working with TALX would give them a competitive edge.

Rick's proposition was not expected, but this wasn't the first time I'd had the happy accident of a solicitation to sell a company I had founded. I've never built a business with the intent to sell it, but in 1970 (Continental Telephone) and 1980 (Citicorp), I answered similar phone calls inquiring about a possible sale. Each time it was an absolute surprise, but I'd learned some valuable lessons in the process that helped when Equifax came knocking.

In 1969, we were thrilled when our fledgling company, Financial Data Systems, reached the one-year mark, because our chances for survival had grown exponentially, and we celebrated with a party for the board and employees at The Cheshire Inn. Statistically, most new businesses fail within the first few years, but everyone on the FDS team had dedicated themselves to growing the business and had worked tirelessly to keep us from becoming a statistic.

Things had continued to go well for us in the second year; we'd grown our staff and customer base at a steady clip. In 1970, we had just celebrated our second anniversary at Financial Data Systems when we got that first call. It was from Ed Whitter from Continental Telephone. He said he'd heard good things about us. He wanted to come by and learn more about what we were doing. Continental was the third-largest telephone company in the country. The corporate headquarters were in St. Louis. We thought that getting a compliment from their upper management was quite flattering.

We were happy to talk to Ed. His approach was so disarming, and still being a young company, we were willing to share just about anything he wanted to know. Ed listened intently as we talked about our business and revenue model, our plans for growth, and went as far as sharing our challenges and needs.

He filled a few pages of his notebook and then left. I thought to myself, *Well, that was nice,* and then went about my business.

I hadn't thought twice about the meeting with Ed until a week or two later when he called to ask for another session with us. He said he wanted to have another conversation, and he wanted to bring with him Phil Lucier, Continental's president. During the meeting, they gave us a high-level view of Phil's plans to push Continental into the emerging technology market. They were purchasing several smaller computer and software companies that looked promising, with the goal of creating a technical business arm that complemented their robust telecommunications business. Ed was scouting companies for acquisition, and we'd been on their radar as a potential candidate. That's why he'd met with us the first time.

I thought Phil Lucier's ideas were visionary, and, as far as we knew, no one else was doing it at the time. Computer companies, like FDS, had just begun dipping their toes into online communications and relied on telephone lines to connect their systems. Telephone companies, like Continental, were moving away from corded switchboards and increasing their reliance on technology to do business. The partnership made a lot of sense to us, and we were excited about what Continental was doing. Ed asked if we wanted to discuss being a part of the initiative.

Now, at the time, the financial risks for FDS were evident, and Bill Corrington and I were still new to the entrepreneurial game. Though things were promising, there was definitely a sense that we were perched on the end of a limb.

Bill and I thought about it, and we had a few more conversations, after which Continental came to us with a $3 million buyout offer, payable in stock. When we started Financial Data Systems, we never thought about how much money we'd make. We were just excited to start something, and our instinct was that we would be successful. The offer astounded Sally and me. We couldn't believe the perceived value when they put a dollar amount on what we'd created.

We didn't build FDS to sell it for millions; we were solving a problem for First National Bank and other financial institutions. We didn't launch into The Work Number with the intent of making billions; we were solving a problem for human resource departments and creating a revenue stream to keep the company viable. I enjoy solving business problems with technology. If someone wants to pay money to control the solution I've created, I'm willing to listen.

Bill and I accepted Continental's offer. I learned a lot about the way to approach acquisitions from this deal, and in particular the need to build a relationship with a company before delving into your intent to buy them.

With the prospect of additional income, Sally and I began house hunting. Our home on Cheyenne Court held fond memories, but Jim and Tom needed some room to stretch out, and we knew it was time to move on. Sally was looking for an old, white farmhouse to decorate with antiques, and I wanted to find a big, stone house. We struck gold when we found what we both wanted at 620 North Taylor in Kirkwood, Missouri. The old two-story, white-stone house was minutes away from our parents, but far enough from Webster that it didn't feel too close. There was ivy choking the mortar outside and chipping, peeling woodwork and flooring inside. With its 1930s kitchen, it was definitely a fixer-upper, but it had character. It was the right size for our family, and Sally and I fell in love with the guts of it. I negotiated the price down so we could put more resources into fixing it up, and we closed on the house for around 25 percent less than the listing price.

The ink had barely dried on the buyout contract when tragedy struck. It was a call from Continental Telephone. Phil Lucier was leaving from lunch at the Pierre Laclede Building in Clayton, and as he opened the driver's-side door to get in his car, it exploded, killing him instantly. It was a tragic and shocking headline, and everyone doing business with Continental, including us, got a call from the FBI. To this day, I don't know if they ever solved the case.

As news of Phil's death reached us, we wondered what this meant for our new relationship, realizing it was probably not good. Still, everyone was shocked when Walter Metcalfe, a friend of mine today and an investor and attorney for FDS, was called by the Continental lawyer, and was told the deal was off. Walter and I agreed, since we had a signed a legally binding agreement, that we were going to hold their feet to the fire. Walter set out to push the contract through, and the next few days were tense for Sally and me with our newly signed mortgage. How were we going to get out of that if the deal fell through? After a few days, Walter came back with a revised contract, changing the structure of the payout to $2 million in stock up front. The remaining $1 million in stock would be paid if we met a certain profit margin in the first eighteen months. I believe Walter pulled off a miracle!

When the contract was signed and the deal was behind us, we tried to get back to the way things were. Continental, without Phil Lucier and his vision, wasn't interested in our business, nor in managing it. With the help of our sixty employees, we were able to make our profit margin well within the period of the contract. Continental began selling off their tech acquisitions a year later. The management team that was running the company at the time didn't have the same vision as Phil Lucier had. I had taken several accounting courses in college and was familiar with the principles of acquisition accounting. In a stroke of divine circumstance, I happened to learn that Continental had used the "pooling of interests" method of accounting for the acquisition of FDS. That meant that on Continental's books, FDS was evaluated at the par value of the stock the shareholders had received, a very small number. (This method of accounting is no longer available for companies that acquire other businesses.) I realized that if Continental received just over the value on their books on the FDS sale, they could show a profit for the divestiture. So Bill Corrington and I, along with the original FDS stockholders, were able to repurchase FDS, with no questions asked. We paid a bargain basement price, about seven cents on the dollar of the original deal. We got this amazing deal because there were no other interested parties. Business and profits grew after we took the reins back. We expanded by adding data centers in Buffalo, Schenectady, and Boston. We did this with the lead customer, a savings bank, of each data center providing the capital needed. We had built a strong recurring revenue data service business. Seven or eight years later, we got a telephone call from Citicorp that resulted in the second sale of FDS. Again, I didn't look back.

The final sale of FDS to Citicorp and later the sale of TALX to Equifax weren't filled with as much intrigue and tension as the Continental deal. Between repurchasing the company for pennies on the dollar and being able to build it up enough to make a sizable profit again, the deal ended up better than we could have expected.

The Final Sale to Equifax

In May of 2007, I stood at the podium at another TALX shareholders' meeting, this time to approve a billion-dollar-plus sale of TALX to Equifax. This last sale, combining two public companies, was quite different from earlier sales, and, in some ways, it was the easiest. A lot of energy was spent keeping the transaction confidential before contract signing and public announcement. We used the code names "Pujols" for TALX and "Chipper" for Equifax, representing my favorite Cardinals baseball player, Albert Pujols, and their favorite Atlanta Braves player, Chipper Jones. These code names were used in all communication, both verbal and written, in secret meetings, and in the bargaining terms!

As I looked over the crowd at this meeting, I realized what a journey we'd been on. I was very emotional. I was proud of all that TALX had accomplished but humbled by the response. Someone in the audience asked what the deal meant for our operations moving forward. I told them I had a three-year contract that I expected to fulfill. Equifax wanted TALX to stay on course.

TALX had grown from twenty-five original employees to approximately two thousand employees. Every $9 share was now worth well over $150, due to the buyout. Our database exceeded 200 million employed people's records. In my wildest imaginings, I never would have believed this could happen.

Chapter 14
THE TALX WAY

FDS was absolutely singular in its culture. I say this because I learned from former employees that it felt like Camelot, but at TALX, I had come to know my faith better, and we had run the business using the Christian principles I had learned along the way. Nothing else could compare to it. TALX had exceeded FDS in every aspect as a quality business and workplace. We had an excellent business model and a pristine character that I don't believe anyone could find in those West Coast dot-coms dominating the tech industry. This was the American Dream for the entire TALX team of employees and for me. At a company celebration at our offices, I received a round of applause and cheers from my employees. There was a line of people thanking me for bringing the company to the next level, and some more personal thank-you notes for helping people professionally grow their careers.

The employees gave me a framed photo of "Fred Bird," the Cardinals Mascot, sitting in my office chair, kicked back with his feet up on my desk. It really made me laugh. And then they presented me with a plaque containing photos of everyone at all of our offices nationwide, with "Fred Bird," again at the top, with the inscription, "Thanks for taking us to the next level," above the date of the sale, May 15, 2007. That one brought tears to my eyes.

As you have read in this book, the TALX culture was a nurturing, encouraging one with an underlying principle of freedom to fail. Employees that left TALX to work for different companies would often come back and visit. Most of them agreed in their comments comparing their current work atmosphere to the TALX culture, indicating the uniqueness of what they experienced at TALX.

Below are several aspects of the culture that contributed to that uniqueness. They are by no means original, but, in combination, they created a somewhat original working environment.

1. **The "FISH" customer service program**, created by Steven C. Lundin, PhD

    This is a philosophy that is communicated through training classes, films, and a book entitled *FISH*. The program is adaptable to many areas of an organization. We initially used it to train our customer service staff on an innovative way to improve our customer service. I was so enamored with it that I personally adopted it in my dealings with the entire company and people I would meet. Even my family noticed those changes in my life.

FISH has four principles. I will not describe them fully here but will list them to encourage you to learn more about the program. Use Google for a start.

- **Choose Your Attitude** each day before you set out
- **Play,** have fun
- **Make Their Day,** how can you accomplish this with each encounter
- **Be There,** be fully present, focused on others' needs

The two principles that had the most impact on me were **Choose Your Attitude** and **Make Their Day.**

2. **Setting Achievable Goals**. We set goals each year per the business plan outline discussed earlier. We made sure that the goals were realistic, meaningful, and achievable. There was an **annual bonus system** in place for the staff members responsible for the goal to reward achieving and exceeding the particular goal. Achieving a goal is both motivating and rewarding.

3. **Grace Abounds: Freedom to Fail**. In my view, one should not shy away from an idea or an opportunity to innovate just because it might be seen as trivial, or the boss might not like it. There was some of that attitude in the company's

culture. I knew that I couldn't be the source of all innovation. The best ideas in an entrepreneurial organization percolate upward, directly from customers' needs through our staff.

I felt a need to communicate this to all. One thing I hoped for from all of our employees was that they would do their jobs well. I wanted them to have the freedom to think outside the box to solve problems and create efficiencies. An organization grows on fresh ideas. But that's not always easy for employees to do, and it's not difficult to understand why. The majority of people don't want to make mistakes. They have an inordinate fear of failure, so they never step out with a new idea or take the initiative to champion anything innovative.

I realized that one practical habit I could implement was based on the principle of grace, which is God's unmerited favor. God granted me forgiveness for my failures, and this empowered me to a greater faith. The idea of passing grace along to others, to empower them to fear less, became a passion.

Therefore, when we had a problem that needed to be discussed and resolved, we would have a meeting and "put the failure on the wall," writing it on the board or a flip chart. I would begin the meeting by saying, "Grace abounds. You are forgiven." Then we would treat the failure as a group problem. No one person was singled out as the guilty party. I wanted all of us to feel responsible not only for the problem, but also for the solution. That encouraged the "freedom to fail" environment that gave people confidence to be creative and innovative at TALX.

4. **Applicant Testing.** We tested all applicants with personality and aptitude measuring tools. Next there were a series of interviews, possibly up to five, with peers, supervisors, and people from other departments that the applicant might interact with. An applicant might end up talking with me, especially someone who might touch our customers, as the last interview. All of this indicates a fairly rigorous hiring process. When a new hire came to work, everyone knew they had passed through the same rigorous steps as the rest of the employees. The new person was readily accepted and welcomed into the TALX family. One of my business principles is this:

People like to work with people they like, and customers will buy more from people they like.

5. **Management by Wandering Around (MBWA).** I enjoyed getting out of my office and visiting with employees. I learned a lot and could often respond to help them solve problems. When on my walks, I was relaxed, with no schedule. I believe that made me more real, and consequently people were not uncomfortable talking to the CEO. My office door was seldom closed, so people could drop

by and say hello. I not only welcomed that; I enjoyed the personal contact.

6. **Positive "Can Do" Attitude.** I had one myself and encouraged everyone to have the same. It is part of the "Choose Your Attitude" from *FISH*.

7. **Celebrate!** Celebrate a sale by ringing a bell. Celebrate an important goal achieved with an employee meeting. Celebrate your team's home opener with a barbecue. Celebrate birthdays with a cake. Celebrate employee anniversary milestones at regular meetings. Celebrate outstanding achievements with a dinner, celebrate with popcorn Thursdays. We purchased a popcorn popper, and every Thursday the Popcorn Committee would make popcorn for all the employees to come and enjoy.

Celebrate!

Chapter 15
HANGING UP MY SPIKES

Several years after the Equifax sale, it became clear that it was time to slow down. I had always been active and energetic, and for seventy-one years I had run, played sports, and worked out. All of that took its toll over time, and by the end of 2009, I had undergone two back surgeries in five months to fuse my lower five lumbar vertebrae. I thought I would recover more quickly than I did, but my energy, focus, and mobility were zapped. The surgery had left me with minimal muscles below the knees of both legs, and I had "foot drop" in both my feet. I had difficulty walking. That became a permanent condition, but by strengthening other muscles, I am able to get around adequately, just not gracefully.

In May of 2010, I woke up one morning and said to myself, "I just don't have the energy to do what I'm doing anymore."

Surprisingly, it was a simple decision. Rick Smith, CEO of Equifax, was in our offices for a meeting and I told him that I was retiring in six weeks. I had fulfilled my three-year contract commitment. I knew I needed to distance myself from everything that required a major responsibility so I could spend more time with Sally. Consequently, on June 30, 2010, with my office and desk emptied and my goodbyes said, I walked out of the TALX doors for good. Friends and family were astonished that I could leave it all behind so totally. Most people thought I'd never retire. But it was time. I did it not looking back, but forward. Because—remember—I have no rearview mirror!

Chapter 16

THE SECOND HALF

For twenty-plus years, Sally and I had both been immersed in our responsibilities; me, with a new job at TALX, and Sally as a new teaching leader of a class with Bible Study Fellowship. This period started soon after the boys had graduated from high school and left the house where they had grown up. We became empty nesters, but we had not had much time for each other, as we both took on these major responsibilities. As a Bible Study Fellowship teaching leader, Sally prepared and delivered a weekly one-hour lecture to approximately three hundred women. All the women had prepared their answers to a lengthy set of questions on the scripture passages for the week, which they discussed in small groups. Sally's talk was on the passages they had studied. There were also men's classes, and I attended one for over six years while I was working at TALX.

Sally had her nose in her books, studying and lecturing, and I was often traveling on business, entertaining customers, or distracted by events of the day. Our communication level deteriorated, and the depth of our marriage and relationship suffered.

Retirement changed all that. Sally and I committed to doing new things together. We worked on our bucket list. Immediately, we scheduled a Mediterranean cruise, which we took in May before I retired. It was the first of many. We planned trips to see many of the countries we'd never explored because we'd been so busy with the responsibilities of life.

While on the cruises, Sally and I began playing bridge almost every day, returning to something we enjoyed in high school and college. As a young married couple, when we lived on a tight budget and couldn't afford babysitters, bridge was our primary entertainment. We'd get together with other young couples, especially our friends Ida and Fred Perabo, put the babies to sleep on blankets on the floor, and play bridge on the weekends, and sometimes during the week. When I retired, I decided I wanted to play seriously, and Sally, a little reluctantly, said she would join me if I would help her learn and make it fun. We had committed the next phase of our marriage to doing things together. We began to relearn a game that had become more sophisticated since the 1950s. Only this time it was not social bridge, but competitive duplicate. When we were staying in Naples, Florida, we would go to a bridge center to play. I wondered why St. Louis didn't have a center. Instead they had duplicate games scattered throughout the city at Masonic temple basements, community centers, and churches. In the spring of 2011, I came back to St. Louis determined to investigate and start planning for what would become the St. Louis Bridge Center. Our city was ripe for it. Others had tried previously, but unsuccessfully. This was my kind of challenge . . . another problem to solve.

I visited six centers around the country and spoke to several more on the phone. I then raised the funding from other bridge players in St. Louis, including myself, and created a 501(c)(3) charitable organization, so the donations would be tax deductible. It took a long time, but with my friend and former CFO of TALX Keith Graves' help, we finally found a location with ample parking. What a challenge! After a year and a half of work, on October 1, 2012, it happened! We opened the doors of the St. Louis Bridge Center to around four hundred members. The main goal is to teach people how to play, but the center also hosts at least two games each day of the week for all levels of competition, from beginning to advanced players. Linda Currier, my former administrative assistant who spent hours painting snowflakes for TALX Christmas parties, runs the center and serves lunch for the players each day. Proof of the need and timeliness of the Center is the fact that within four years of its opening, it had become the eighth largest in the country in its volume of bridge players. We had well over seven hundred members. But, more importantly, it has become a significant place for senior citizens, primarily to connect with each other in a safe environment. It has been heartwarming to receive their regular words of thanks and know that I contributed to helping make this time in their lives better.

Bridge was not the only activity that I enjoyed. Several others were approached with intensity, as well. Most were initiated from my entrepreneurial interests:

- In the mid-1970s, I bought a small farm in Washington, Missouri, and began breeding Angus cattle to show and sell. Here was an opportunity for Jim and Tom to learn hard work by having them redo most of the barbed-wire fencing. The farm was also a way to convert my interest in farming from my youth in Ohio to a business model that took advantage of the then-existing tax laws for livestock breeding. As a businessman, however, I didn't fit the mold with the local cattlemen, particularly when I showed up at a cattle show wearing tennis shoes, not cowboy boots. I was referred to as the "Adidas Cowboy" in local cattle breeding circles. I sold the farm in 1985, after the advantageous tax laws were eliminated.

- I played with and worked on model trains as a young boy. As an adult and grandfather of five boys, I wanted to revisit those times. I contracted with a model train builder in Kansas City, Missouri, to build a layout in my basement. After my back surgeries, Sally reminded me that I would not be able to go up and down the stairs very well to "play" with my trains. That model train is now housed in "Canfield Station" at the Magic House, St Louis Children's Museum . It has had far more impact on little boys than just my grandsons. Additionally, during my terms as a board member and Chairman, the Magic House began to fabricate travelling exhibits. The themes of each exhibit were inspired by Beth Fitzgerald, CEO. Beth would find donors to cover the cost. The exhibit would be developed in-house, and then spend a period of months entertaining children in St Louis. The exhibit was then rented to other children's museums around the country. Each exhibit was rented multiple times, creating a nice "recurring revenue" source of funds for the Magic House, once again demonstrating my business principle that is key to the financial success of any organization.

- I love the art of the American Southwest, particularly from the late nineteenth and early twentieth centuries. Some of our walls, both in St. Louis and in Naples, are hanging places for art from the Taos Six, a group of artists who painted in New Mexico and took their art to the East Coast to show easterners what the West was like, and, of course, to sell.

- I began studying wine shortly after we were married. Sally and I now have a six-hundred-bottle wine cellar, and some of our travel is to Napa Valley and the Tuscany region of Italy, to visit wineries and taste the wines of the region. Our sons have followed our lead and also have a real love of wine. It seems they often make small raids on the cellar to augment their collections.

- At the family farm in Washington Court House, Ohio, my aunt Edith raised and trained trotting horses. I enjoyed going to the county fairs and watching the trotting races. I was drawn to the horses. I fed them, watered them, bathed them, and walked them to cool off after a training session or race. As an adult in my sixties, I got an itch to own a thoroughbred racing horse. I researched the several ways to acquire one and landed on the concept of syndication, in which several people invest in the same horse, providing ownership, but at a lesser risk. I studied the various syndicating companies and picked Team Valor, because of their record of success. The owner/manager of Team Valor is Barry Irwin, a very smart guy. Barry has a unique approach to picking horses for his syndicate. He looks first at the confirmation of the horse, then at the pedigree, not vice versa. After a few years of experience of buying several of Barry's recommendations, I stumbled onto an idea that brought some success to my racehorse investments. That was the concept of investing primarily in female horses, because (1) a male horse was generally more expensive than a female, and

(2) I learned that a male horse who had failed was worth far less than a failed female horse. The female could possibly become a mare and have babies. The failed male was usually sold immediately to stop using up cash for maintenance fees. So I stopped investing in males. The result of this strategy is that one of the foals of a mare I owned 15 percent of became a successful racehorse. His name was Animal Kingdom, AK for short. Because I owned 15 percent of his dam, I also owned 15 percent of AK. I had no significant investment in this colt. AK won the Kentucky Derby in 2011, he was second in the Preakness, second in the Breeders' Cup Mile, and went on to win the Dubai Derby. The Dubai Derby's purse is the richest in the world. AK retired and was sold into stud in 2014. I am still cashing checks from AK's new life as a stud.

- Around the year 2000, we began to spend a week or ten days in the winter in Naples, Florida, staying with friends, Harold and Sonny Helmkampf. We loved Naples, and not wanting to impose on the Helmkampfs for a longer time, we invested in a condominium. We owned that for seven years before we started looking for a house, with Larry and Mary Catherine White, our real estate agents. We wound up buying a "remodel" in Old Naples at 180 Eighth Avenue S, a block and a half from the beach, and convenient to Fifth Avenue shops and restaurants, as well as Third Street restaurants. We hired an architect, Matt Kragh of MHK, to design a "cottage look," desiring to return to the home style of Naples prior to the "Tuscan" building era. After several iterations, we approved the plans and hired Waterside Builders, whose owner is Mike Assaad, to build our home. Mike and Matt had worked on several jobs together before. We were so pleased with the result that at the completion celebration, I asked the "team," Matt, Mike, and the Whites, if they wanted to do this again. They all agreed. So, with this team, I have become a developer, and to date, the team has purchased, torn down, designed in cottage style, built, and sold six single residential homes in Old Naples.

- Sally got into the entrepreneurial spirit when she joined two other women and formed Ivy Cottage Antiques. Sally has always loved antiques and the quest to find a treasure. Several of our vacations were to New England, where quality antiques, especially furniture, can be found. The trio travelled on their own antique hunting trips on many occasions. They did not have an antique shop. They would buy, and in some cases refinish, mark up, and sell at various antique shows in the Midwest. Not being as interested in antiques as Sally, I knew I needed to support her passion. So, I got involved in collecting Toby mugs and stoneware crocks decorated with birds and flowers. Many of these grace our home today.

Chapter 17
DOGGIN' IT!

It's worth mentioning that, along the course of our married life, Sally and I had five dogs and no cats, much to Sally's disappointment, as she grew up with cats and no dogs. But I'm allergic to cats, thus the problem. In many ways, the stories of our five dogs reflect a bit of our own life history during those times.

Our first dog at North Taylor, probably around 1976, was Nickel (Nicky), an adorable Old English sheepdog, which our neighbors convinced us we would love, because their wonderful dog Penny had had puppies. Sally, with no dog experience, inherited the job of dog care. Nicky drove her crazy because she loved to run after people as soon as she hit the front yard. Living on a busy street like North Taylor created a big safety problem for the dog. I loved the dog, but she was work. She had to be brushed almost daily, trained, fed, walked, and watched like a hawk. She didn't seem to understand "come" or "no." That was a huge problem!

I left on a business trip when the dog was six months old, and when I came home, it was to *no* Nicky. Sally had had it! She had given the dog away.

Our second dog was a little white mutt called Mogie (for Mogul because we were into skiing by that time). We only had him for a few years because he misbehaved. We often chained him to a pole outside. That seemed to reduce Sally's responsibilities of walking the dog, but not being educated dog people, we were unaware that the chaining was a bad idea. One day, Mogie bit a neighbor boy. We did not realize that the neighbor kids often teased and taunted poor Mogie when he was chained. The biting was a logical response, but that was the end of Mogie.

Our next puppy was Sally's impulse purchase. She and her friend Karen visited a farm where a litter of puppies just happened to be weaned and were available, for free, to a new home. You guessed it. She and her friend couldn't resist and both came home with black female puppies of unknown pedigree. They named them Maggie and Glory. This time it was because both Sally and her friend Karen were in Bible Study Fellowship, studying the book of John. Maggie was named for Mary Magdalene and our puppy was named Glory for the

Glory of God. But our puppy was no Glory. She was a disaster. She was hyperactive and chewed, nipped fingers, tinkled in the house, and never learned to mind or behave. Sally even took her to dog training, but this puppy was incorrigible. We eventually found a home for her on a farm where she could run free. I cut Sally a little slack at the time for bringing Glory home because her mom was dying of congestive heart failure and had moved into our home for her final days. Glory enjoyed jumping around on Maw Maw's bed as a puppy and making her smile. But it wasn't long until she *had* to go!

We waited many years until we were ready for a dog again. This time, I did research and got a golden retriever puppy we called Bucky (named after the Ohio buckeye because my brother and I had gotten involved in managing our family farm in Ohio). Bucky was a ten on a dog scale of ten. Our boys adored him, and he was a great family pet. Even though Sally had issues with Bucky's shedding and tinkling occasionally in the piano room, she loved him too, and even took on his care when the boys opted out. We only had him for nine years, as he contracted cancer and died far too soon. Losing Bucky was tough, but the boys were off to college soon and Sally said she had had enough dogs for a while—a long while!

Then we had a surprise—sort of like a woman discovering she is pregnant at age fifty. I had begun to ask Sally about getting a dog again. It had been twenty-five years since Bucky, but she said an unequivocal *no*! I kept gently agitating until she finally got upset with me and said, "Listen, Bill. I don't want a dog. If I did, it would be a little cuddly lap dog that didn't shed. Not a big one like you want. But the truth is that I don't want any dog. *No* and *no*!" That curt response kept me quiet for a few months, but I really wanted a dog. So I started to make subtle suggestions again, venturing into the subject with measured caution. That brought a fierce response from my wife: "Bill, I'm tired of this discussion. Please know that if you are dead set on having a dog, it's the dog or me!" Well, I hadn't expected such a strong a response and I knew she wasn't really serious, but it did make the point, again, that she meant *no more dogs*! I made light of it and told her that today I was still choosing her, but that it would be a daily decision that could change at any time. We both laughed at what became an ongoing family joke, but with a touch of seriousness.

One day, we were invited to a fundraising auction at Covenant Christian School by our friends Dave and Linda Yates. During dinner, various auction items were paraded through the room for all to see. Two eight-year-old girls carried a little black puppy that fit into the palms of their hands. Our friends had them drop this puppy in Sally's lap. They knew the *no more dogs* story. I could see Sally melt as I noted that this was a small, no-shed, hypoallergenic lap dog. Bingo! I decided a little dog was better than no dog, so when bidding was well underway for the puppy, I asked Sally if she wanted her. She cautiously nodded her head. Success! I knew this puppy had her heart and I was going to get my dog—finally, after twenty-five years.

I vigorously outbid all opposition and we had a Yorkshire terrier/poodle mix, called a Yorkypoo, to take home. Only, we were not prepared. We had had no plans to take a dog home. There was prep to get ready for such a big event, so we arranged to pick the puppy up a day later. She came home to become the best dog we'd ever had. I never thought a dog could top Bucky, who was truly a man's dog. But this little bundle of silky soft black fur wormed her way into my heart and onto my lap immediately. I had thought I was getting what Sally wanted but found myself equally engaged with what would become an eight-pound bundle of personality and affection. We called her Allie after Albert Pujols. The Cardinals had just won the 2011 World Series with Pujols as one of the stars. Today she is eleven years old and the delight in our home. We saved the best for last!

Chapter 18
GRATITUDE ATTITUDE

*"Honor the Lord with your wealth,
with the first fruits of all your crops."*
—Proverbs 3:9

Sally always made sure we gave to church from the very beginning of our marriage. As our resources grew, I got the feeling it was important to give more back. Not only was it something I'd read in scripture, but consequently, something that God was calling me to do. When I was able to increase the amount of time, talent, and treasure we shared with organizations, it was hard not to notice what we received in return. Not in any kind of material way, of course, but it is gratifying to know that you've been able to do something significant for God's Kingdom with the resources with which you have been blessed. Giving became a major part of our life around two decades into our marriage and has been an essential part of our family ever since.

Sometimes giving is narrowly defined as writing a check. Sometimes that is the best we can do but being able to recognize when your talent and time are needed can be the bigger gift. That was the case when a group of parents of kids from Kamp Kanakuk got together and decided to find a way to bring home the Christian principles taught at the camp. Kanakuk was instrumental in helping Sally and me discover our Christian faith. We thought we were Christians all of our lives, but when we visited this camp, we began to understand the lifestyle of Christianity in a whole different way: First Kanakuk and then immersion in the scriptures. Together they had produced a revelation for our family in helping us understand the Bible's role as a guide for faith and practice.

Joe White, president of Kanakuk Kamps, and a group of moms were instrumental in helping to create the first chapter of K-Life, which opened in St. Louis in 1980. Although not yet a Christian, I was the first board chairman and president, only because none of the other parents involved knew how to organize a new venture. We met as couples, and our goal was to hire a young couple to be our K-Life leadership team. We would provide them with a place to live and a salary to support them. As board members, we all were expected to give, and we were going to use fundraising to supplement the organization's budget. Sally and I opened the apartment above our garage to house the K-Life staff. For over thirty years, that little apartment housed young people in ministry: in K-Life and others. What fun to partner with God. Today, K-Life has thirty-one chapters in cities across the United States, and it recently launched a new, urban K-Life chapter, the second in St. Louis, to reach out to inner city kids and their families.

It was in the 1980s that our calling to give beyond tithing became stronger. Several events in our life encouraged us to "dig deeper." One was a quick decision to go to Poland on a two-week mission trip with Campus Crusade (CRU). Moved by the missionaries we met in Krakow and Warsaw, along with a sobering visit to Auschwitz, we came home deeply impacted by the trip. Our priorities began to shift as we desired to be more involved in building God's Kingdom.

Sally and I created a foundation supporting Christian education for children and adults. Westminster Christian Academy, the Magic House, and Central Christian School are among the beneficiaries. I have served on boards helping ministries develop staff and broker acquisitions to help them expand. Westminster, where my grandchildren attended high school, was able to purchase a large tract of land and build a new secondary school. The Magic House was able to raise significant donations for an endowment, as well as a much-needed expansion, doubling its size. Sally and I were able to help in these, not to bring credit to ourselves but to honor God. Consequently, we prefer that most of our gifts are anonymous.

We have been exceedingly blessed in business and in life. I have learned that all that I am and have belongs to God, so our giving is a right response to what He has done for us. We can't begin to out-give Him.

A family Thanksgiving. 2016

*In the back yard of the house our children grew up in.
That's our dog Bucky in front, who is no longer with us. 1982*

Bill and Jim playing 3-D checkers during a Colorado ski trip. 1974

Bill and Walter Metcalfe at Washington University's Outstanding Alumni award ceremony, at which Bill was honored. Walter was the guest speaker. 2001

Bill with grandchildren Becky and Eddie. 2000

TALX was listed on NASDAQ in 1996, but this picture was taken on September 10, 2001—one day before 9/11.

Bill and Sally on opening day. 2006

Tom and Jim, CODASCO varsity baseball. 1982

Sally and Bill's wedding, September 2, 1961.

Mom and Dad in Ireland. 1983

Annie's graduation at the University of South Carolina, May 2018

Sally and Bill. 2018

www.ingramcontent.com/pod-product-compliance
Lightning Source LLC
Chambersburg PA
CBHW052057110526
44591CB00013B/2244